For Isadora
We all need a little magic in our lives.
May you one day find your horse-loving, leading man.

Bomber Bases of
World War 2
2nd Air Division
8th Air Force USAAF
1942–45

AVIATION
HERITAGE TRAIL SERIES

Bomber Bases of World War 2 2nd Air Division 8th Air Force USAAF 1942–45

Liberator Squadrons in Norfolk and Suffolk

Martin W. Bowman

Pen & Sword
AVIATION

First published in Great Britain in 2007 by
Pen & Sword Aviation
an imprint of
Pen & Sword Books Ltd

Copyright © Martin W. Bowman, 2007

ISBN 978 1 84415 547 7

Typeset in Palatino by
Phoenix Typesetting, Auldgirth, Dumfriesshire

Printed and bound in England by
CPI UK

Pen & Sword Books Ltd incorporates the Imprints of Pen & Sword Aviation,
Pen & Sword Maritime, Pen & Sword Military, Wharncliffe Local History,
Pen & Sword Select, Pen & Sword Military Classics and Leo Cooper.

For a complete list of Pen & Sword titles please contact
PEN & SWORD BOOKS LIMITED
47 Church Street, Barnsley, South Yorkshire, S70 2AS, England
E-mail: enquiries@pen-and-sword.co.uk
Website: www.pen-and-sword.co.uk

Contents

Acknowledgements

When an inquisitive teenager armed with a Kodak Instamatic first chanced upon the lurid murals, pin-ups and cartoon characters in the early seventies they looked fresh and colourful. Swords had long been turned into ploughshares and many airfields had become industrial estates and the runways used for racetracks or footings for turkey sheds, while some huts housed pigs or stored hay for winter. By the 'noughties' time and the vagaries of the weather had eroded the majority of wall art. Most had faded from grace, some had lost their lustre completely, but their aura lives on in a few Nissen huts and barrack blocks of the desolate bases of Norfolk and Suffolk. Even now, fresh discoveries are made that keep alive these fields of Little America. East Anglia had a great preponderance of airfields, many of which had been built during the 1930s expansion period for use by RAF Bomber, Fighter and Coastal Command squadrons in time of war. With America's entry into the conflict in late 1941 some stations were soon taken over by the USAAF but many more were needed for the Eighth Air Force. Air Ministry and American engineer battalions cut a swathe through the furrowed fields of Norfolk, Suffolk and Cambridgeshire, leaving in their wake airfields destined for use by bomb wings and fighter groups. At first the USAAF had only seventy-five airfields in the United Kingdom but the total eventually reached 250, costing £645 million, £40 million of which was found by the American government.

For me their rediscovery led to exploration, research and finally, a host of books on the American air forces in East Anglia and further afield.

I would like to thank Mike Bailey, BBMF, CONAM; Pat Everson, Wiley S. Noble, 3rd SAD Association; Pat Ramm, Ben Jones, John Gilbert, the staff of the 2nd Air Division Memorial Library, Norwich; Steve Graham, 669 Squadron AAC; the late John H. Woolnough; and everyone who kindly loaned photographs.

Introduction

In America in the 1930s one of the main theories about strategic air power was that heavily armed but unescorted formations of long-range bombers could fight their way through to a target in broad daylight and destroy the objective with precision bombing. This theory was taught at the Army Air Corps Tactical School at Maxwell Field, Alabama, and precision bombing was honed to perfection at ranges in California's Mojave Desert in 1940 using the top-secret Norden bombsight. Experienced bombardiers soon found that they could place their practice bombs within yards of the target from as high as 20,000 feet which led to claims that bombs could be dropped in a pickle barrel from such heights. With America's entry into the Second World War General Ira C. Eaker's VIIIth Bomber Command was established in Great Britain with a few B-17 Flying Fortress and B-24D Liberator bomb groups in East Anglia. When USAAF missions began in earnest the *Luftwaffe* day fighters now had to drive the heavily armed and armoured American bombers from the skies by co-ordination of fighter formations and closed formation attacks.

By the end of August 1942 over 100 B-17s, enough for three groups, had arrived in the United Kingdom. On 17 August, the Eighth Air Force flew its first mission of the war when a handful of Fortresses were dispatched to north-eastern France, where they bombed a large marshalling yard. B-17 crews threw

1

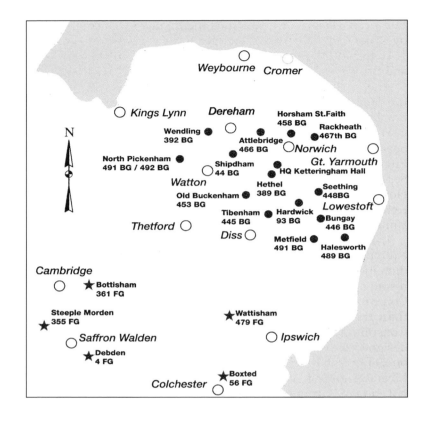

themselves headlong into a bitter war over Europe in daylight and without escort, despite opposition, particularly from the US Navy, which was convinced that America's first objective lay in the defeat of Japan. In September 1942, plans to introduce the B-24 Liberator into Europe were fulfilled when the 2nd Bombardment Wing (which was to grow into the 2nd Bombardment Division and later the 2nd Air Division) was established in England.

The 2nd Air Division was activated at Detrick Field, Maryland, as the 2nd Bombardment Wing, on 7 June 1942. It was redesignated the 2nd Bombardment Division on 13 September 1943 and it became known as the 2nd Air Division on 1 January 1945. During its assignment to the Eighth Air Force in the

European Theatre of Operations the division was commanded by Major-General James P. Hodges from 7 September 1942 until 1 August 1944, Major-General W. E. Kepner until 13 May 1945, and Brigadier-General W. H. Peck, from 13 to 31 May 1945.

After a short period of training at Detrick Field the cadre of the Headquarters and Headquarters Squadron of the 2nd Bombardment Wing moved to Fort Dix, New Jersey, then to the port of embarkation, where the liner *Queen Elizabeth* was boarded for the trip across the Atlantic. They arrived at their first English station, Camp Thomas, at Old Catton in Norwich, on 7 September 1942. Later the headquarters (HQ) moved, first to Horsham St Faith airfield nearby and then, in December 1943, to Ketteringham Hall, where it remained until its departure for the United States in June 1945.

The 2nd Air Division's fourteen bomb groups were wholly equipped with the B-24 Liberator bomber throughout its tour of duty in East Anglia in the Second World War. The Liberator had resulted, early in 1939, from a request from the US Army Air Corps to design a heavy bomber of infinitely better performance than the Boeing B-17 then in production. As a result, the Consolidated Aircraft Corporation of San Diego, California, designed the Model 32 and the Liberator flew for the first time on 20 December 1939. An attempt to re-equip all England-based Liberator groups with the Fortress never materialized because not enough Fortresses were being built and in contrast, Liberator production was phenomenal. During 1942 Convair opened a second Liberator production line at Fort Worth, Texas. A third production line was brought into operation at Tulsa by the Douglas Company, and at the end of 1942 a fourth was opened by the Ford Motor Company at Willow Run. In early 1943 North American at Dallas, Texas, operated the fifth and final major factory manufacturing Liberators.The B-24 surpassed the production of every other single type of American military aircraft during the Second World War. In all, 18,188 examples were built (5,000 more than the total Fortress production).

The first mission flown by units under the command of the 2nd Bombardment Division was on 7 November 1942 and the final mission was flown on 25 April 1945. In addition to missions flown from its East Anglian bases three groups (44th, 93rd and 389th) participated in three campaigns while based in

North Africa. One of these, 93rd Bomb Group had flown in two campaigns in North Africa during the previous winter. The 2nd Air Division developed into an extremely powerful striking force. In addition to its fourteen bombardment groups, it had five fighter groups. On 7 August 1944 the 492nd Bomb Group was withdrawn from combat, having lost fifty-four aircraft in May–July 1944. This was the heaviest loss for any B-24 group for a three-month period. The 491st Bomb Group moved from the 45th Combat Wing (CBW) to take the place of the 492nd in the 14th CBW. Crews were dispersed throughout the rest of the Eighth. The 491st, late of the 45th CBW, took over at North Pickenham, the 492nd's previous base, and began operations with the 14th CBW. The 491st's former 45th CBW partner, the 489th, was transferred to the 20th CBW. The 2nd Bombardment Division now totalled an unlucky thirteen groups and remained at that number until November 1944 when the 489th was rotated to the USA, on paper at least, for redeployment to the Pacific as a B-29 outfit.

On 28 August the 20th Wing groups were converted to a transportation role in support of the Allied ground forces in France, who were in urgent need of fuel and supplies. When the Allies launched Operation *Market Garden* using British and American airborne divisions against German-held Dutch towns on the Rhine in mid-September, the Liberators were once again called upon to supplement the troop carriers.

Losses continued to rise. On 27 September 1944 the 2nd Bomb Division put up 315 Liberators, including thirty-seven from the 445th, to raid the Henschel engine and vehicle assembly plants at Kassel in central Germany. For the 445th Bomb Group it was one of the most tragic and probably the most disastrous raid for a single group in the history of American air warfare. The 445th Bomb Group lost no fewer than twenty-five Liberators in the space of just six minutes, and five more crashed in France and England. Only five made it back. The plant's destruction was well received by Eighth Bomber Command, which estimated that six to seven weeks' production would be lost. On 26 November, when over 1,000 Fortresses and Liberators escorted by fifteen fighter groups headed for the synthetic oil plant at Misburg near Hanover, the 491st Bomb Group lost sixteen Liberators. Total B-24 losses this day were twenty-one while fifty-three returned battle damaged and with fifteen crew Killed In Action.

The 2nd Air Division's maximum total strength was 8,870 officers and 43,884 enlisted personnel. In all, a total of 95,948 sorties were flown on 493 operational missions by the bombardment groups of 2nd Air Division. A total of 199,883 tons of bombs was dropped on enemy installations in all parts of Europe, from Norway in the north to the shores of the Mediterranean in the south and from Poland and Romania in the east to the shores of the Atlantic in the west. Its gunners claimed 1,079 enemy fighters destroyed in combat while 1,458 of its B-24s were lost on operations and 6,032 airmen killed. The division was awarded six Presidential Unit Citations and five individuals received the Medal of Honor for heroism displayed while flying in combat as members of its groups.

Between 1942 and 1945 there were, at any one time, around 50,000 USAAF personnel, including nearly 200 members of the Women's Army Corps, stationed within a 30 mile radius of Norwich. Approximately 3,000 servicemen lived on each of the fourteen airfield bases close to village communities. Here populations were suddenly to increase from no more than 200 souls to the size of a small town. Close friendships developed and persist to this day between members of the 2nd Air Division and local people.

CHAPTER 1

The Eighth Air Force Bombing Offensive 1942–45

In England in September 1942 seventeen B-24D Liberators of the 93rd Bomb Group established themselves at Alconbury in Huntingdonshire. The 93rd remained in the shadow of Fortress operations for some time and it was not until 9 October that the group flew its maiden mission, to the Fives-Lille steelworks in Belgium. This was the first mission flown by the Eighth Air Force from East Anglia, and over 100 bombers participated. Colonel Ted Timberlake, commanding officer (CO) led twenty-four B-24Ds to the target behind the much larger formation of B-17s. The group lost a B-24 over France and only ten Liberators hit their target. At the end of the month the 93rd lost two of its squadrons on detached duty to Coastal Command, scouring the Bay of Biscay for U-boats. During October various echelons of the 44th Bomb Group equipped with B-24D Liberators, arrived at Shipdham airfield in Norfolk after crossing the treacherous northern Atlantic. It fell to these two B-24 groups and four B-17 groups to prove conclusively that daylight precision bombing could succeed in the deadly skies over Europe. The RAF remained unconvinced and in November 1942 even American instructors doubted their crews' ability to bomb in daylight and survive against German opposition. Experience won the hard way on early missions resulted in modifications to the Liberator's armament in Northern Ireland. Fifty-calibre machine-guns were installed in the vulnerable nose section to combat the head-on approach favoured by *Luftwaffe* fighters. Automatic belt feed systems were introduced on all machine-gun armament, replacing the cumbersome process of changing drums containing only thirty-six rounds by hand. Enterprising armament officers concocted their own field modifications, installing 'twin-fifties' in the 'glass-house' area, which were fired by bombardiers and navigators lying on their stomachs. The *Luftwaffe* soon developed a healthy respect for the new armament and reverted to conventional pursuit tactics. Losses mounted. The Liberator, with its operationally high wing-loading, made it a difficult aircraft to maintain in formation above 21,000 feet although its service ceiling was put at 28,000 feet, about 4,000 feet below the optimum Fortress altitude. In addition, the B-24D's operational cruising speed of 180 mph was between 10 and 20 mph faster than the B-17's. This caused countless problems in mission timings and usually the Liberators were relegated to the rear of the B-17 formations and consequently soaked up all the punishment. The problems caused by the difference in speed and altitude of the B-24 and B-17 were only finally solved when the Fortresses and Liberators flew missions separately from one another.

On 29 May the 44th and a few 93rd Liberators, hastily withdrawn from night operations to bolster the flagging fortunes of the 'Eightballs' were withdrawn for low-level training for a raid on the Ploesti oil refineries in Romania. In early June the 44th, 93rd and recently arrived 389th Bomb Groups flew low over East Anglia almost every day. After a series of raids in support of the Torch Operation, Ploesti was attacked from Libya on Sunday, 1 August 1943, when the USAAF mounted *Tidal Wave*. On this day the oil refineries of Ploesti in Rumania were the targets for 177 B-24Ds of the 8th (44th, 93rd and 389th Bomb Groups on temporary duty (TDY) from England) and Ninth Air Force (98th and 376th Bomb Groups) flying from North Africa. Malfunctions and accidents *en route* reduced the effectiveness of the Liberator force and navigational errors caused severe problems in the target area, forcing some groups to bomb each other's assigned targets. Some 167 B-24Ds actually attacked their targets, dropping 311 tons of bombs on the Ploesti refineries. Forty-four B-24Ds were lost. Three B-24s crashed into the sea. Eight B-24Ds were interned in Turkey, while nineteen landed in Cyprus, Sicily and Malta. Of the ninety-two that returned to North Africa, fifty-five were battle damaged. At least thirty-three Liberators were downed by flak and ten by German, Bulgarian and Romanian units, for the loss of ten German and fifteen Romanian fighters.

When the three groups returned to England later that month Liberator B-24H and J models with power-operated nose turrets had appeared with the arrival of the 392nd Bomb Group at Wendling. This fourth B-24 group heralded a new era for the Liberator in Europe and was soon joined by the 445th, 446th, 448th, and 453rd groups, all equipped with the H and J models. Even so the division was still not strong enough to mount deep-penetration raids without fighter escort.

The New Year began with the famous General Jimmy Doolittle taking over command of the Eighth Air Force on 1 January 1944. His directive was simple: 'Win the air war and isolate the battlefield!' In other words: 'Destroy the *Luftwaffe* and cut off the Normandy beaches for the invasion.' Operation *Argument*, which quickly became known as 'Big Week', took place during the week 20–25 February, with massive raids on aircraft plants in Germany and Austria. Losses were high and on 24 February when 239 B-24s headed for the Messerschmitt Bf 110 assembly plant at Gotha, the 445th Bomb Group lost thirteen B-24s and six 389th Liberators were also lost. Both the 445th and 392nd Bomb Groups were later awarded Presidential Unit Citations for their part in the raid. On 25 February the USSTAF brought the curtain down on 'Big Week' when 1,300 Eighth and Fifteenth Air Force (AF) bombers and 1,000 fighters were despatched to aircraft plants, ball-bearing works and components factories throughout the Reich. The 2nd Bombardment Division (BD) bombed the Me 110 component plant at Furth. Less than a week after 'Big Week', the USAAF launched its first attacks on 'Big-B' – Berlin.

By March 1944 the 2nd BD had grown to eleven groups with the addition of three new groups, the 458th, 466th, and 467th, making up the 96th CBW. On 1 April 246 B-24s headed for the chemical works at Ludwigshafen. Thick cloud over France meant only fifty-four continued to the target while 162 bombed targets of opportunity at Pforzheim and Grafenhausen. Some thirty-eight bombers in the 44th and 392nd Bomb Groups veered off course and bombed a Swiss town in error. The incident led to America having to pay the Swiss thousands of dollars in reparations. It was not until 8 April that the cloudy conditions abated and allowed the Eighth to assemble in force. Some thirteen combat wings consisting of 644 bombers were dispatched to aircraft depots throughout western Germany, including 192 bombers, which attacked Brunswick. A total of thirty-four heavies were shot down during the day's missions. Thirty of these were Liberators, of which eleven were from the 44th Bomb Group and six from the 466th Bomb Group. The majority of the losses came down in the area of Brunswick due to persistent fighter attacks.

On 13 April overall command of the Combined Bomber Offensive and the 8th AF officially passed to General Dwight D. Eisenhower, newly appointed Supreme Allied Commander. Operation *Cover* called for raids on coastal defences, mainly in the Pas de Calais, to deceive the Germans as to the area to be invaded by the Allied armies massing in Britain. On 6 June 1944, D-Day, a total of 2,362 bomber sorties, involving 1,729 B-17s and B-24s, was flown, dropping 3,596 tons of bombs for the loss of three Liberators (two of which collided over France). The VIIIth FC flew 1,880 sorties and claimed twenty-eight enemy fighters shot down. US ground crews worked throughout the night of 6 June and all day on the 7th so that two missions could be flown. Tactical targets in France continued to be attacked until 15 June. From July to September all five B-24 groups in the 3rd Division converted to the Fortress and many Liberators found their way into 2nd Bombardment Division groups.

It seemed that the war would be over by Christmas but on 16 December 1944, using appalling weather conditions to his advantage, Field Marshal Karl von Rundstedt and his *Panzer* formations supported by an estimated 1,400 fighters, attacked American positions in the forests of the Ardennes on the French-Belgian border. They opened up a salient or 'bulge' in the Allied lines, while in England the Allied air forces were grounded by fog. It was not until 23 December that the heavies could offer bomber support in the Battle of the Bulge. On Christmas Eve a record 2,034 8th AF bombers, including weary hacks and even assembly ships, and 500 RAF and 9th AF bombers took part in the largest single strike flown by the Allied air forces in the war, against German airfields and lines of communication leading to the "Bulge". Overall, the Christmas Eve raids were effective and severely hampered von Rundstedt's lines of communication. The cost in aircraft, though, was high. Many crashed during their return over England as drizzle and overcast played havoc with landing patterns. Tired crews put down where they could. Only 150 aircraft were available for another strike on 26 December. Next day the wintry conditions were responsible for a succession of crashes during early-morning take-offs. On 29 December runways were covered with ice, and snow and fog added to the treacherous conditions. Despite this, Command decided that the mission in support of General Patton's forces near Metz was so imperative that it must go ahead. At Rackheath, near Norwich, four out of five Liberators that took-off on instruments were lost.

On New Year's Day 1945 the 2nd BD was redesignated the 2nd Air Division. Meanwhile, many ground staff on the East Anglian bases were transferred to the flagging infantry fighting in the Ardennes, and disabled and injured men arrived to take their place. All at once the 'general bitching' ceased as many realized how much better off they had been than their counter-parts in France. Missions continued, weather permitting, and the position in the Ardennes gradually swung in the Allies' favour. By 3 February 1945 Marshal Zhukov's Red Army was only 35 miles from Berlin and the capital was jammed with refugees fleeing from the advancing Russians. Accompanied by 900 fighters, 1,200 B-17s and B-24s dropped 2,267 tons of bombs on the centre of Berlin, killing an estimated 25,000 inhabitants and destroying 360 industrial firms, heavily damaging another 170. At the Yalta Conference early in February 1945, Josef Stalin, the Russian leader, and his army chiefs asked that the RAF and 8th AF paralyse Berlin and Leipzig and prevent troops moving from the west to the eastern front. British Prime Minister Winston Churchill and American President Franklin D. Roosevelt agreed on a policy of massive air attacks on the German capital and other cities such as Dresden and Chemnitz. These cities were not only administrative centres controlling military and civilian movements but also the main communication centres through which the bulk of the enemy's war traffic flowed. The most devastating raids of all fell upon the old city of Dresden in eastern Germany, starting with an 800-bomber raid by the RAF on the night of 13 February. Two waves of heavy bombers produced firestorms and horrendous casualties among the civilian population. Next day 400 bombers attempted to stoke up the fires created by RAF Bomber Command while 900 more bombers attacked Chemnitz, Magdeburg and other targets. On the 15th over 1,000 heavies bombed the Magdeburg synthetic oil plant and next day almost 1,000 B-17s and B-24s hit oil targets at Dortmund, Salzbergen and Gelsenkirchen.

On 22 February *Clarion*, the systematic destruction of the German communications network, was launched. More than 6,000 Allied aircraft from seven different commands were airborne this day and they struck at transportation targets throughout western Germany and northern Holland. All targets were selected with the object of preventing troops being transported to the Russian front, now only a few miles from Berlin. Despite the low altitudes flown, only seven bombers were lost. Next day only four bombers were lost from the 1,274 despatched, and on 26 February only three bombers were shot down over Berlin.

By March 1945 the systematic destruction of German oil-production plants, airfields and communications centres had virtually driven the *Luftwaffe* from German skies. In Germany the now desperate situation called for desperate measures to be taken against the all-powerful bomber streams and last-ditch attempts were made by the *Luftwaffe* to try to stem the tide. One plan was the deliberate ramming of American bombers by converted Bf 109 fighters, flown by pilots of *Sonderkommando Elbe* called *Rammjäger*. On 7 April the *Luftwaffe* employed the *Rammjäger* fighters against American bomber streams attacking underground oil refineries in central Germany and destroyed seventeen aircraft. Throughout early April Me 262 jet fighters were seen regularly by Liberator crews. Fortunately, lack of fuel and a shortage of pilots to fly the revolutionary fighter kept their incursions to a minimum. The 8th AF retaliated by bombing their airfields, but only the end of the war ended their threat completely.

On 14 April an estimated force of about 122,000 Germans holding out and manning twenty-two gun batteries along the Gironde estuary in the Royan area, were bombed by 1,161 heavies. The 467th successfully dropped all their 2,000-pound bombs within 1,000 feet of the MPI; half the bombs falling within 500 feet. This was a bombing pattern unsurpassed in 8th AF history. The 389th Bomb Group lost two Liberators when 3rd Air Division B-17s, making a second run over the target, released their fragmentation bombs through their formation. Two more crash-landed in France and a fifth limped back to England. On 15 April nearly 850 heavies of the 2nd and 3rd Air Divisions (ADs) carrying Napalm for the first time, dropped 460,000 gallons in 75–85 gallon liquid-fire tanks on the stubborn defenders of Royan. The 1st AD added 1,000 and 2,000 pound GP bombs while three fighter groups put down fire on gun emplacements. No Flak was encountered and French forces later captured the port.

During the week of 18–25 April, missions were briefed and scrubbed almost simultaneously as the ground forces overran objective after objective. The end came on 25 April 1945 when 282 B-24s, escorted by four fighter groups, bombed four rail complexes surrounding Hitler's mountain retreat at Berchtesgarden. During the first week of May the German armies surrendered one by one and finally to Eisenhower at Rheims in the early hours of 7 May. VE (Victory in Europe) Day took place on 8 May. The bomb groups returned Allied prisoners of war (PoWs) to England and France, and airlifted displaced persons from all over Europe. Then *Trolley* or *Revival* missions in bombers crammed with ground personnel were flown at heights ranging from 1,000 to 3,000 feet over bombed-out cities to show them the outcome of Allied bombing over the past four years. On 13 May 1945 a victory flypast was flown over the 8th AF Headquarters at High Wycombe. From the middle of May to the end of July all thirteen 2nd AD Liberator groups returned to America via Wales and the Azores.

CHAPTER 2

The Airfields

ATTLEBRIDGE (STATION 120)

Attlebridge airfield, which is in the parish of Weston Longville, was built during 1941–2 by Richard Costain Ltd for operation as a satellite airfield for Swanton Morley in RAF 2 Group which operated light bombers. As such the runways were 1,220, 1,120 and 1,080 yards long. In August 1941 Blenheim IV light bombers of 88 Squadron arrived from Swanton Morley and in September these aircraft were replaced by Boston III aircraft. No. 88 Squadron moved to Oulton in September 1942 and the base was transferred to the 8th AF 2nd Bomb Wing, although the first American flying units were the 437th and 438th Squadrons of the 319th Bomb Group, which arrived with Martin B-26B Marauders in October. These remained for just a month before leaving for the 12th AF in North Africa, although a few Marauders remained until March 1943 when the airfield was used by 320 (Dutch) Squadron, RAF, flying B-25 Mitchells. The Flying Dutchmen departed in August 1943 as the base was destined for 8th AF heavy-bomber use although rocket-firing Typhoons and then some war-weary PB4Y-1 Liberators of the US Navy were based here for a time. Several small, country roads were closed and the airfield was greatly enlarged for heavy bomber use. The main east-west runway was extended to 2,000 yards and the two others extended to 1,400 yards. The

13

perimeter track was also extended and hardstandings increased to fifty. Part of this construction work was undertaken by an engineering detachment of the US Training Command from Colorado, although work was not fully completed until two years later, when the number of men at the base totalled almost 3,000. Towards the end of 1943 plans had been made for Attlebridge to receive the 466th Bomb Group commanded by Colonel Arthur J. Pierce, and to this end the 61st Station Complement Squadron arrived to administer the base. During February 1944 the B-24H Liberators of the 466th Bomb Group flew in to Attlebridge after completing periods of training in New Mexico, Utah and Kansas. The ground echelon sailed for the UK in March.

The 466th flew its first combat mission on 22 March when the Liberators went to Berlin. Two of the Group's B-24s, Second Lieutenant William Terry's 41-29434 *Terry and the Pirates* and Second Lieutenant Gilley T. Brand's 41-29416 *Rebel Yell*, collided. Next day the 466th lost two more Liberators in another collision when over Holland 42-52587 *Shoo Shoo Baby* flown by Second

Major Glenn Miller and Colonel John H. Woolnough pose for a photo at Attlebridge during the bandleader's visit in August 1944. (John H. Woolnough)

Aerial view of Attlebridge airfield in April 1946 with the village of Weston Longville (top right) and Greengate (top centre). (USAF)

Attlebridge control tower in 1944. (John H. Woolnough)

Winter scene at Attlebridge in 1944–45. The control tower is just
visible to the left of the centre of the picture. (John H.
Woolnough)

Lieutenant Robert L. Garrett and 41-29466 *Dark Rhapsody* piloted
by Lieutenant Donald C. Griffin went down *en route* to the
target, the German airfield at Achmer. Sixteen men in total were
killed. On 24 March the 466th went to St Dizier before being
stood down for two days. When the group resumed missions on
27 March there was a thick haze at Attlebridge at take-off time
and assembly was difficult. B-24H 41-29364 *Star Dust* and
42-52562 collided shortly after take-off over Hoe. One of the
Liberators crashed at Northhill Green while the other crashed at
Gorgate Hall. All twenty-four men plunged to their deaths. This
third fatal collision took the group's losses to six in five days,
hardly an auspicious start to life in the European Theatre of
Operations (ETO). There were other accidents during the
group's combat tour. On 17 June 1944 at 0220 hours an acci-
dental burst of machine-gun fire from a B-24 on a hardstanding
set fire to B-24 42-51093 which was completely destroyed. On 25
July 1944 B-24H 41-29402 *The Mad Monk* hit trees on take-off and
made an emergency landing at RAF Swanton Morley. By the end
of hostilities the 466th had lost twenty-four Liberators to various
causes and forty-seven missing in action.
    In all, the group flew 232 operations, during which they

On 18 August 1944 six Liberators of the 466th Bomb Group, including B-24D 41-24109, the striped assembly ship (formerly *Ready and Willing* of the 93rd Bomb Group, seen here with T9-D, also from the 784th Squadron), flew the famous American band leader Major Glenn Miller and his band from RAF Twinwoods Farm airfield just outside Bedford to the 355th Fighter Group base at Steeple Morden, Cambridgeshire, for an afternoon concert. Later that afternoon Glenn Miller and his band were flown to Attlebridge to play an evening concert for the 466th Bomb Group's 100th mission party. Miller returned to Steeple Morden on 26 August to give another concert, this time at the 355th Fighter Group Officers' Club. (D. Crow/Richards Collection)

dropped over 12,900 tons of bombs. One of the greatest successes came on 11 June 1944 when the 466th and the other two groups in the 96th CBW destroyed the important railway bridge over the Loire River at Blois-Saint-Denis from low level. The bridge was destroyed which earned the wing a citation from 2nd Bomb Division HQ. The 785th Bomb Squadron also distinguished itself by flying fifty-five consecutive missions without loss. Less distinguishably on 4 March 1944 the 466th Bomb Group bombed Basle in Switzerland in error during a mission to a target about 44 miles away. The 466th was stood down for two days while an enquiry and subsequent court-martial ensued. Some of the group's missions were to deliver fuel to the Allied armies on the continent during eleven days in August 1944 when the B-24s of the 96th CBW flew 2,117,310 gallons to France in 5-gallon jerrycans, aircraft drop-tanks and bomb-bay containers.

The 466th departed from Attlebridge on about 6 July 1945 and the base reverted to a satellite to 25 Maintenance Unit (MU) RAF, Great Ashfield, and was known as 94 Maintenance Sub-Unit. The airfield runways and Hockering Woods nearby were used to store bombs until August 1948. Up until December 1980 several of the wartime buildings remained, including a blister hangar and the control tower, while a number of smaller buildings were used by local farmers. Attlebridge airfield was sold between 1959 and 1962 and Bernard Matthews Ltd, the largest integrated turkey company in Europe and probably the world, began using the runways for turkey-rearing operations and the buildings for administrative purposes.

BUNGAY (FLIXTON), (STATION 125)

This airfield was first planned as a satellite for Hardwick airfield and Kirk and Kirk Ltd began construction in 1942, building three intersecting runways, fifty dispersed hardstandings and two T2

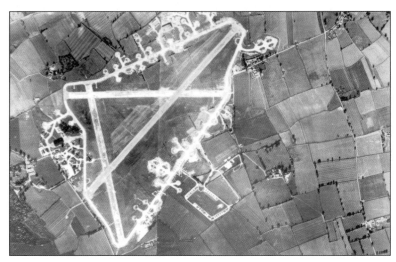

Bungay (Flixton) airfield in October 1945. (USAF)

hangars plus the usual technical, administration and domestic buildings to house nearly 5,000 men. First to use the airfield, in October and November 1942, were the 428th Bomb Squadron of the 310th Bomb Group, USAAF, equipped with B-25C Mitchells. These were followed on 3 December by about eight crews of the 329th Bomb Squadron of the 93rd Bomb Group, which were equipped with B-24D Liberator bombers. Their task was experimental involving 'intruder' or 'moling' flights over Germany in an attempt to disrupt working schedules in German factories by causing air-raid warnings to sound, upsetting civilian morale and impairing industrial output. The first intruder mission was undertaken on 2 January 1943 when four Gee-equipped B-24s took off for various parts of the Ruhr. Radio transmitters spaced at intervals throughout Great Britain beamed out given radio signals, which were picked up by the Gee-carrying bombers. The time lag between the signals received, after certain calculations, indicated the B-24s' exact position. Operating singly, because of the flight's experimental nature, the 329th lost the concentrated

B-24H *The Worry Bird!* of the 707th Bomb Squadron, 446th Bomb Group at Bungay (Flixton) following a raid over Germany in 1944. This aircraft was salvaged on 15 October 1944 after damaging its nose section in a taxiing accident on the base. (Art Livingston)

firepower that formation flying afforded it. However diminishing cloud on this first mission forced the Liberators to return to Flixton. Six more attempts were made – the last on 28 March 1943. Many sorties had to be aborted due to insufficient cloud cover, which was an essential requirement for this type of operation. The project was subsequently abandoned and the 329th left Flixton to take part in conventional bombing missions after the secret equipment had been removed. The experience had been rewarding, however, and some crews later formed the nucleus of the USAAF Pathfinder units set up to perfect blind-bombing techniques.

Now another heavy bomb group – the 446th – appeared on the scene. In October the group's ground echelon departed for Camp Shanks, New York and sailed for Scotland aboard the *Queen Mary* before continuing their journey to Bungay. The air echelon meanwhile, had departed for England via the southern ferry route. The CO, Colonel Jacob J. Brogger, and his crews arrived at Flixton on 4 November minus one of the Liberators, which was shot down while *en route*. Flixton airbase was bare and inhospitable, partly constructed and short of facilities when the Americans arrived. By April 1944, when construction was completed, there were 2,826 men at the base, including 363 officers. Early days were spent listening to mandatory lectures

The technical site at Bungay (Flixton) airfield in 1944. (USAF)

and completing training in every aspect of flying combat missions in the ETO. 'The Bungay Buckaroos' as they became known, flew their first mission on 16 December 1943 when the target was Bremen. On returning two B-24s crash-landed on or near the base and were written off. This was followed by a mission to Osnabrück on 22 December, when the first losses were sustained over enemy territory.

The 446th Bomb Group flew a total of 273 combat missions from Flixton, during which they dropped 16,800 tons of bombs and lost fifty-eight Liberators in action and twenty-eight to other operational causes. The 'Bungay Buckaroos' took part in 'Big Week' – the concerted attacks on the German aircraft industry – in late February 1944. On the mission to the Messerschmitt Bf 110 plant at Gotha on 24 February the Bungay group suffered two losses out of a total of thirty-three lost by the 2nd Bomb Division. Second Lieutenant Cecil T. Miller of the 704th Bomb Squadron brought his crippled B-24 back with a badly holed port wing. The crew, with the exception of the pilot, co-pilot and navigator, baled out ever Flixton. Miller headed for the emergency runway at RAF Woodbridge but while he was circling the airfield all four engines died from lack of fuel. Miller ordered the two crew still aboard to bale out and he steered the B-24 away from some barrack huts before crashing at Hill Farm, Sternfield. Miller died in the crash and he was subsequently awarded a posthumous Silver Star.

The mission to the Hamm marshalling yards on 22 April 1944 was postponed until late in the day and caused the 2nd Division groups to return at dusk with navigation lights on. A surprise follow-up by Me 410s of KG51, which hit the Waveney Valley groups during their let down for landing caused chaos in the area. In the night's confusion, twelve Liberators crashed or crash-landed in Norfolk and Suffolk. Thirty-eight American crewmen were killed and another twenty-three injured. Two Me 410A-1s were claimed shot down. Although Flixton airfield was attacked, no known losses were sustained. On 27 April 1944 the increased hours of daylight allowed the group to fly two missions. B-24H 42-50306 had just cleared the runway when the wind suddenly veered and the pilots lost control. The aircraft crashed near Abbey Farm, Flixton, and the bomb load exploded soon afterwards killing the crew of ten.

Flixton's greatest moment was probably on 6 June 1944 when the 446th had the distinction of leading the 8th AF on the first mission of D-Day. By 1400 hours the Liberators at Flixton were formed in two lines converging at the head of the runway. This avoided the problem of anyone leaving a revetment, going off the runway and ruining the timetable. All aircraft had their navigation lights on with the yellow-orange assembly ship, *Fearless Freddie*, completing the scene, taking off first at about 0200 hours to form the group. Colonel Brogger was flying with Lieutenant Charlie Ryan of the 704th Bomb Squadron in *Red Ass* renamed, for public relations purposes, the *Buckaroo*. However, the first over the beaches would be *Liberty Run*, one of the 564th Bomb Squadron, 389th Bomb Group's 14 Pathfinder Force ships used on D-Day. Following a lengthy assembly the 446th formation hit the Normandy beach defences at H-hour minus 3 (5.55) on D-Day and was followed by three more missions flown by the 20th CBW in support of the landings. The following weeks saw the 446th employed in mainly tactical missions until the land forces were firmly established in France before missions were flown to a number of 'Crossbow' (V-weapons) sites and other targets.

Commencing at the end of August 1944 the group was employed occasionally on 'trucking' operations – flying in much needed supplies to France. On 18 September the 446th took part in the low-level supply drops in Holland in support of the airborne forces at Nijmegen. During this mission the group lost three Liberators and twenty-five out of the thirty-six taking part were damaged. Colonel Brogger was wounded, and he was subsequently decorated with the Silver Star. Command of the 446th then passed to Colonel Troy W. Crawford, who remained as CO until 4 April 1945. On that day he was flying as command pilot for the mission to a jet airfield at Wesendorf near Dortmund in a 'Red Tail' Mosquito of the 25th Bomb Group employed for formation-monitoring duties. Unfortunately, a B-24 gunner who mistook the twin-engined British aircraft for an Me 262 shot it down. Crawford baled out and was captured but he later escaped with forty others to the Allied lines. He arrived back at Flixton on 25 April and then returned to the USA. Probably the most tragic accident of all occurred on 11 April 1945 as the 446th Bomb Group returned from an attack on

Halesworth (Holton) airfield in October 1945 during RAF
occupation. (DoE)

Regensburg. Two B-24s, 42-50790 *Funny Face* and 42-51907,
collided in mid-air while circling the base and crashed at
Mendham and Homersfield with the loss of twenty-one lives.

One of the most famous Liberators served in the 446th Bomb
Group. B-24H 41-29144 *Ronnie* of the 704th Bomb Squadron,
which was named in memory of Staff Sergeant Ronald Gannon,
a waist gunner who died of paralysis during the group's training
programme in the USA. Master Sergeant Michael P. Zyne in the
704th Squadron took charge of the B-24 after it had been plagued
by mechanical difficulties on its first four missions with another
squadron. Zyne's crew despatched *Ronnie* on its first successful
mission on 5 January 1944. It flew its 100th mission on 30
December 1944 and its 105th in January 1945 and finished the
war with an ETO record of seventy-nine consecutive missions
without a turn back. The 706th and 707th Bomb Squadrons were
credited with over sixty consecutive missions without loss.

The 446th's last raid was flown on 25 April 1945 and the
group left for the USA in July. The base was handed over to
the RAF on 20 July 1945, becoming No. 1 Sub-Site of 53
Maintenance Unit (Pulham). During the winter of 1945/6 the
station became HMS *Europa*, being the satellite of HMS
Sparrowhawk (Halesworth), where three Fleet Air Arm

squadrons were based. With the departure of the Fleet Air Arm Flixton was transferred to RAF Maintenance Command and it became a maintenance sub-unit of 94 MU with its HQ at Great Ashfield. Stored on the runways and in buildings were 250, 500, 2,000 and 4,000 pound bombs, balloon-cable cutting cartridges, depth charges, 7 inch parachute flares and German ammunition. The latter two items were eventually taken to 53 MU Pulham and destroyed there. About July 1949 the site was taken over by 53 MU until its closure in 1955.

HALESWORTH (STATION 365)

Though this airfield was built near the village of Holton it took its name from the market town of Halesworth to the east. Construction of the airfield began in 1942–3 and three runways were laid, the main one being 2,000 yards long and the two others 1,400 yards long, with fifty-one hardstandings. Two T2 hangars were erected and Nissen hut accommodation built for 3,000 men, being dispersed mainly in Holton Park south of the flying field. Although the airfield was intended from the outset for use as a bomber station, it was only 8 miles from the Suffolk coast and ideally situated, therefore, for fighter escort missions, where range was the most important consideration. In July 1943 the 56th Fighter Group and its eighty P-47C and D Thunderbolts arrived at Halesworth from Horsham St Faith. Part of the 65th Fighter Wing, the 'Wolfpack' as it was popularly known, comprised three squadrons: the 61st, 62nd and 63rd (coded HV, LM and UN respectively) and was commanded by Colonel Hubert Zemke. The group was to become the highest-scoring American fighter outfits by the war's end, with over 670 aerial combat victories and more than 500 destroyed on the ground. The number of aces (five or more victories) was also the highest in the 8th AF and included pilots such as Francis Gabreski, the leading 8th Air Force ace, with twenty-eight victories, Robert Johnson (twenty-seven) and Walker H. Mahurin (twenty-one), while Zemke himself was credited with eighteen. The 56th Fighter Group's first real success came on 17 August 1943, the day of the first Schweinfurt and Regensburg missions, when they shot down seventeen enemy fighters without loss. With the use of drop tanks the range of the P-47s was greatly extended so that on 4 October they were able to provide escort as far as Frankfurt, where fifteen Bf 110s were claimed shot down. In early November 1943 the 56th was the first group to be credited with 100 victories. While escorting a bomber mission to Bremen on 26 November twenty-three *Luftwaffe* fighters were destroyed for the loss of one Thunderbolt, the pilot of which baled out safely over Holland. By the spring of 1944 the 56th Fighter Group's total score had reached 250. With the approach of D-Day all five of the 9th AF's fighter groups in the Colchester area were moved to Kent and on 18 April 1944 the 56th Fighter Group were transferred to Boxted to be nearer to the Continent.

5th ERS ASR OA-10A Catalinas, in co-operation with RAF high-speed launches and Warwicks, rescued hundreds of downed airmen in the North Sea during the latter part of the Second World War. On 23 March 1945 three OA-10As were on ASR patrols and they rescued six RAF airmen, including Pilot Officer Strafford, navigator with 612 Squadron, seen here being lifted from Catalina 44-33915 at Halesworth after being rescued from off the Dutch coast. (Charles J. Johnson via Theo Boiten)

A B-24 Liberator of the 489th Bomb Group, over the Schulau oil refinery near Hamburg on 6 August 1944. (USAF)

During the first fortnight in May the 489th Bomb Group, which had been activated on 1 October 1943 and equipped with B-24H and J Liberators and was commanded by Colonel Ezekiel K. Napier, flew in from the USA. The 489th, together with the 491st Bomb Group at nearby Metfield, were to form the 95th CBW, which had been activated on 11 December 1943. This was the fifth and final wing of the 2nd Bomb Division and unique in that it was the only one with two groups, the other four each had three. The 489th ground echelon had sailed across the Atlantic on 13 April and the aircrews began flying the southern ferry route to England in May. On 29 May the 489th flew a practice mission over Major-General Hodges' 2nd Bombardment Division HQ in tight formation and next day it flew its first mission when it bombed Oldenburg airfield in Germany. The group crossed the Dutch coast 10 miles south of their briefed target, where an accurate flak barrage enveloped them and a navigator was killed. On the homeward leg Second Lieutenant Edwin T. Clark, pilot of *No Nookie Now,* was forced to ditch in the North Sea after running low on fuel and he and seven of his crew were rescued and made PoWs.

A practice mission had been scheduled for midday on 2 June but crews were later told that the 489th would join with the 491st for a raid on Bretigny airfield near Paris in the first full 95th Wing mission. Forty-one B-24s took off from Halesworth to rendezvous with thirty-six Liberators of the 491st. The 95th Wing reached the CP on schedule but the lead aircraft in the 489th decided to ignore the briefed dog-leg route which avoided the flak on the southern side of Paris and instead fly straight to the French capital. The formation rolled up their bomb bays, opened up their throttles, and at 19,000 feet headed for the primary target. The main force, led by the 489th, continued over the centre of Paris to Creil airfield while fourteen others bombed Villeneuve airfield in mistake for Bretigny. Heading home again the 489th forsook the briefed route and four Liberators were lost to flak over northern France while others sustained varying degrees of damage. At Halesworth three liberators crashed and had to be written off.

Missions continued to France and on 4 June. *Sack Rat,* piloted by Second Lieutenant Clifford R. Galley of the 491st Bomb Group, developed a high-speed stall while forming up and crashed near Sizewell in Suffolk, killing everyone on board. On Monday 5 June 629 bombers attacked coastal defence installations in the Cherbourg-Caen and Pas de Calais areas, together with three No-ball sites and a railway bridge. Six B-24s, including *Missouri Sue* (a 44th Bomb Group PFF ship), which carried the 489th Bomb Group deputy commander, Lieutenant-Colonel

Leon R. Vance, were lost. A malfunction prevented bomb release on the target, a V-1 site near Wimereaux and, despite protests, Vance ordered the crew to go around again. This time the bomb drop was made by hand but two bombs hung up. Now the flak had increased in intensity and an 88 mm salvo burst directly under the port wing. Captain Louis A. Mazure, the pilot, was killed instantly when he was hit in the temple and Earl L. Gamer, co-pilot was seriously wounded. Three engines were put out of action and *Missouri Sue* rose menacingly on the verge of a stall.

The tall, rangy, colonel, who was standing behind the pilots' seats, looked down to see that his right foot had been virtually severed from his leg and was attached only by the Achilles tendon, which was jammed behind the co-pilot's seat. Despite his terrible injury, Vance managed to reach the panel and feather the three useless engines. Gamer cut all four engines and turned the B-24 towards England. When the shoreline came into view Lieutenant Bernard W. Bail, the radar navigator, ordered the crew to evacuate the B-24.

Although he was suffering from shock, Bail managed to get the colonel down into his navigator's seat. He took off his belt

Leon Vance with his daughter Sharon in front of the B-24
named in her honour. (USAF)

and wound it around Vance's thigh to stop the blood spurting. His quick thinking undoubtedly saved Vance's life. Bail told him they would have to jump because there was no way they could land the B-24, especially since the two bombs were ready to go off on impact. The colonel shook his head and said he would not jump. Bail knew that he could not possibly drag Vance to the bomb bay and push him out, and he was also aware that the aircraft was rapidly losing altitude. There was little time left to save himself. Bail checked the tourniquet one last time, shook Vance's hand, and jumped from the open bomb bay. Vance managed to get into the cockpit, and succeeded in ditching within reach of the English coast. The impact blew him clear of the aircraft and he was quickly picked up by Air-Sea Rescue (ASR) and given immediate medical attention.

Vance was awarded the Medal of Honor, the fifth and final airman in the 2nd Bomb Division to receive the award and the only one who was crewman flying from England (the other four all being awarded for actions at Ploesti in August 1943). Vance underwent amputation of his right foot, and was later invalided home in a C-54. Somewhere between Iceland and New-foundland the Skymaster, with its crew and patients, disappeared without trace. (Bail was later shot down, on a mission to Stuttgart, his twenty-fifth operation, and made a PoW.)

The 489th flew its 106th and final mission on 10 November before being taken out of combat operations and disbanded. During their six month at Halesworth the 489th had dropped nearly 7,000 tons of bombs at the cost of twenty-nine B-24s missing in action and twelve written off through other oper-ational causes. Crews and aircraft were sent to other groups as it was intended that the 489th would be re-formed in the USA as a B-29 Superfortress unit to be sent to the Pacific to fight the Japanese. However, the war ended before they became oper-ational again.

In mid-January 1945 the 5th Emergency Rescue Squadron (ERS) arrived at Halesworth from Boxted. This was an independent unit controlled by the 65th Fighter Wing of 2nd AD which supplemented the RAF ASR service in recovering ditched aircrew from thin North Sea and English Channel. Aircraft included about twenty-five war-weary P-47Ds, which had been retired from active fighter groups, modified to carry 150 gallon belly tanks, a dinghy pack on each wing, and four smoke markers. They were thus equipped to search, locate and render immediate assistance to ditched crews until the arrival of rescue craft. A few all-white OA-10 Catalina amphibians with greater endurance than the P-47s were also used. B-17G *Donna J II*, fitted to carry an airborne lifeboat, operated from Halesworth during March and April 1945 on detachment from the 457th Bomb Group. One of the lifeboats was dropped to a ditched crew off Denmark. During their period of operation the 5th ERS flew over 3,600 sorties, the majority of which were effective.

Two squadrons of the 496th Fighter Training Group, which had been based at Goxhill using P-51s also, operated from Halesworth from 15 February to early June 1945 and were responsible for the indoctrination and tactical training of fighter pilots for the ETO.

The RAF used Halesworth until August 1945, when it was taken over by the Fleet Air Arm (FAA) and became HMS *Sparrowhawk*, with its satellite, HMS *Europa* at Flixton. No. 798 Squadron (Advanced Conversion Unit) arrived from Lee-on-Solent on 6 September with Master II, Barracuda II, Firefly I, Oxford, Beaufort and Harvard IIb aircraft. In early December 762 Squadron (Twin Conversion Unit) arrived from Dale with Beauforts and Oxfords, joined within days by Mosquito TIIIs, FBVIs and B.25s of the recently disbanded 704 Squadron. The General Maintenance Section from Scapa Flow, responsible for supplying and servicing oxygen systems, arrived at Felixstowe in LSTs with their lorries and equipment. At this time about three flyable USAAF P-47s were based at Halesworth. In January 1946, 798 Squadron moved to Hinstock, followed in February by 762 Squadron.

With the departure of the FAA Halesworth became the satellite station of RAF Hethel, under the control of 12 Group, Fighter Command. All flying ceased by February 1947 and for a while the Ministry of Food used the hangars for storage. The airfield was finally sold off in 1963. Most of the land reverted to agriculture; some of the smaller buildings were used by farmers and other firms and a large turkey farm was erected in 1963 on the runways of Le Grys, which was taken over by Bernard Matthews Ltd in January 1976. In 1970 part of the perimeter, together with some newly erected buildings, formed the Suffolk County Council Holton depot.

HARDWICK (STATION 104)

This airfield, which is actually in the parish of Topcroft, was one of the first heavy-bomber airfields constructed in East Anglia. Construction work began in 1941–2 for RAF use and thirty hardstandings were originally built but with plans to turn the airfield over to the USAAF these were increased to fifty to meet their heavy-bomber requirements. A main north–south runway 2,000 yards long and a north-west–south-east and south-west–north-east runways, each 1,400 yards long, a perimeter track and fifty hardstandings comprising thirty-six early 'frying-pan' type and fourteen loops were laid by John Laing & Son Ltd. Three T2

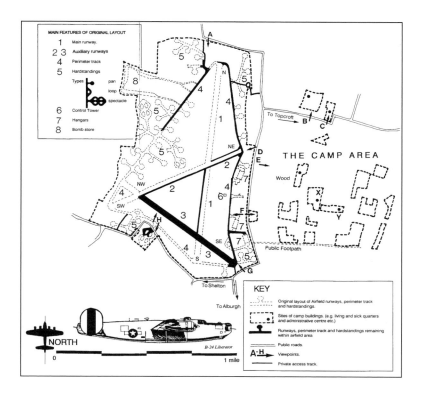

The former control tower at Hardwick airfield. (USAF)

93rd Bomb Group personnel at Hardwick. (USAF)

Colonel Addison T. Baker, CO, 93rd Bomb Group, who was
killed at Ploesti on 1 August 1943. (USAF)

93rd Bomb Group personnel on their English bikes. (USAF)

93rd Bomb Group personnel in the mess at Hardwick. (USAF)

The crew of *Shoot Luke* get ready for a 48 hour pass to London. (USAF)

The arrival of the British tea van at Hardwick gives 93rd Bomb Group ground personnel the opportunity to relax for a few minutes while they sip steaming cups of the traditional British beverage. (USAF)

hangars were erected on the administrative and technical site on the east side of the airfield bordering the country road running from Hempnall to Alburgh. On the eastern side of this road lay the major part of the base, with dispersed domestic sites hidden amongst woodland. Four miles of surface drains, 13 of French drains, 13 of roadways, 5 of sewers and 7 of water mains were laid. A total of 4,750,000 bricks were used in construction of the base. One site was located at Topcroft Street. Accommodation for 3,000 men was of the temporary type, mostly Nissen huts. The bomb dump was situated off the north-west corner of the airfield in and adjacent to Spring Wood.

The first American unit to operate from the airfield was part of the 310th Bomb Group (Medium), which operated B-25 Mitchells from September to November 1942. One squadron was based at the satellite airfield of Flixton. The main party of the 310th had left by late November, although some B-25s and personnel were delayed and were moved to Hethel. On 27 November about eight crews and their B-24Ds in the 329th Bomb Squadron in the 93rd Bomb Group at Alconbury, Huntingdonshire, transferred to Hardwick. Their task was to evaluate the

In the control tower at Hardwick these men perform one of their tensest jobs – totalling the aircraft returning to their base. Others in the control tower are clearing planes on and off field, handling mid-air traffic, weather forecasting and answering crews' enquiries over the radio. With field glasses is Captain L. L. Lebois, Hoboken, New Jersey, and at the window is Major John K. Strobel, New Orleans, Louisiana. (USAF)

RAF-inspired Gee navigational device on behalf of the USAAF, which at the time was considering various RAF operational radar equipment for bombing in overcast skies. However, the squadron moved to Flixton airfield after only a week at Hardwick.

Meanwhile, on 7 December 1942 the 93rd, which was commanded by Colonel Ted Timberlake, had flown to North Africa to participate in raids against Axis ports and shipping for almost three months. In late February it returned to England to be based at Hardwick, where the three squadrons were soon reunited with the 329th. On 22 March 1943 Colonel Timberlake, who was leading his group in *Teggie Ann*, had a narrow escape during the mission to Wilhelmshaven when a 20 mm shell entered the cockpit and missed him by only a few inches. Four days later he assumed command of the 201st CBW (Provisional).

During April 1943 some important visitors arrived in Norfolk. Lord Trenchard, the 'Father of the Royal Air Force', visited

Hardwick airfield, showing (top left) Spring Wood and bomb dump, (top right) Topcroft village, (bottom right) Bush Wood and living sites, and (bottom left) Shelton Common. Living accommodation centred around Topcroft while the MT section is to the bottom left of Bush Wood. Above it is more living accommodation and to its right communal sites. Station HQ is to the right of the two hangars. (USAF)

Station 104 on 6 April and personally congratulated the aircrews. Lieutenant-General Frank Maxwell Andrews, Commanding General of the ETO visited Hardwick on 27 April. One week later, on 4 May, he was killed along with the first crew at Hardwick to complete its tour. Lieutenant Shannon and his crew in *Hot Stuff* crashed into a mountain in Iceland on their way home to America. Only Sergeant George Eisel, the tail gunner, who had escaped two similar disasters, survived after being trapped in the wreckage for fourteen hours. Andrews Field in Essex was named in honour of the late commanding general on 17 May 1943.

Lieutenant-Colonel Addison T. Baker took command of 'Ted's Travelling Circus' as it had become known, on 17 May 1943. On

B-24J-90-CO 42-100294, which was later named *Victory Belle* and 42-100329/A in the 328th Bomb Squadron, 93rd Bomb Group en route to their target. *Victory Belle* and Captain Norman A. Roggencamp's crew FTR on 24 June 1944 when the Liberator crashed at Treon, France. Four men evaded, five were KIA and two were taken prisoner. 42-100329 crash landed on 18 September 1944 and was salvaged two days later. (USAF)

29 May 93rd Bomb Group Liberator crews (along with those in the 44th and 389th) were withdrawn from high-altitude bombing missions and commenced low-level training over East Anglia. At the end of June the three 201st Wing groups (provisional) flew to Libya to take part in a series of raids on Axis targets before participating in a low level strike on the oilfields at Ploesti in Romania on 1 August 1943. The 93rd, led by Lieutenant-Colonel Addison Baker, crossed heavily defended air space and when only a few miles from the target his B-24 *Hell's Wench* was hit and caught fire. Baker jettisoned his bombs but he and his co-pilot, Major John Jerstad, decided to continue to the target. At Ploesti *Hell's Wench* was enveloped in flames and crashed with no survivors. Both pilots were awarded posthumous Medals of Honor for their sacrifice. Captain Walter

Stewart, the deputy leader, in *Utah Man*, took over and despite severe damage to the bomber he managed to land again in Libya fourteen hours later, although K. D. McFarland, flying *Liberty Lad* on two engines, was the last home by another two hours. Nine other 93rd Liberators, including two which collided in cloud, did not return.

The 93rd flew the greatest number of missions of any 8th AF group (340 from Hardwick and forty-nine from North Africa), losing 140 aircraft, 100 of them in action. The much-travelled group was awarded a Distinguished Unit Citation for operations in North Africa from 17 December 1942 to 20 February 1943, and another for its part in the low-level raid on the Romanian oilfields at Ploesti on 1 August 1943.

Hardwick airfield reverted to RAF Bomber Command on 25 June 1945 and was finally closed in June 1962 and then sold. The buildings were soon demolished and part of one runway broken up.

HETHEL (STATION 114)

Early in 1941 Hethel, 4 miles east of Wymondham and 7 miles from Norwich, was a large, flat, and sparsely populated area, which made it suitable for bombers, and the RAF had authorized construction of the base. Work by George Wimpey & Co. Ltd began on 16 August 1942 and was expanded early in 1943 to match the specifications needed to operate the heavy bombers of the 8th Air Force. The Class A type airfield consisted of three intersecting runways; the main south-west–north-east one was 2,000 yards long and the north-west–south-east and west–east ones 1,400 yards. The main runway was also the instrument-landing one and was aligned to the prevailing wind. The width of the runways was standardized at fifty yards and a 50 foot wide perimeter track or taxiway encircled the runway and joined the end of each. Branching off the taxiways were fifty hardstandings (thirty-six pans, eleven loops and two spectacle loops) for the bombers. Three hangars were built on the eastern side. The grounds of Stanfield Hall became the location for the bomb dump. Quarters were built to accommodate 395 officers and 2,679 enlisted men.

Between September and December 1942 Hethel was used by

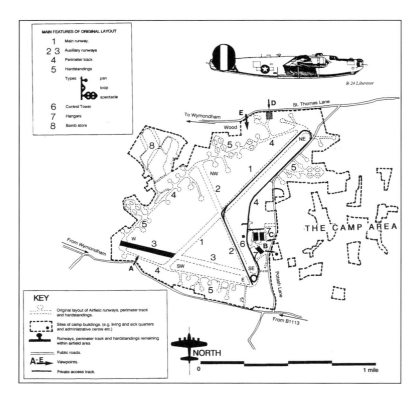

the ground crews of the 320th Bomb Group (Medium) for training before the B-26 Marauder unit left for North Africa. About the same time a squadron of RAF Bostons with a Lysander and Dominie aircraft were based here for a short period. Hethel then became the home of the 389th Bomb Group, commanded by Colonel Jack W. Wood, flying B-24D Liberators and the third group in the 201st Wing (Provisional). After completing a five-day ETO orientation course that emphasized formation flying, the Norden bombsights were removed and replaced with low-level sights and flight crews joined the 44th and 93rd Bomb Groups in low-level flying training at less than 150 feet over Norfolk. On 25 June two 389th Liberators were involved in a mid-air collision.

At the end of June the three 201st Wing groups flew to Libya to take part in a series of raids on Axis targets before partici-

Hethel airfield is transferred from the RAF to the 8th Air Force
on 23 August 1943. (USAF)

pating in a low-level strike on the oilfields at Ploesti in Romania
on 1 August 1943. The twenty-six B-24Ds of the 389th bombed
Red One the Steaua-Romana Refinery at Campina, about 20
miles north of Ploesti. The Campina refinery was so badly
damaged that it would be six years before it again become fully
operational. The 'Sky Scorpions' were the last to arrive over the
target and paid dearly for their lack of surprise. Of the twenty-
nine B-24Ds that bombed the target six did not return to Libya.
Two went down at the target, two more crash-landed in
Romania and two flew to Turkey and were interned. Second
Lieutenant Floyd H. 'Pete' Hughes and co-pilot Lieutenant
Ronald Helder, flying *Eager Eagle*, pressed home the attack and
Lieutenant John McLaughlin, the bombardier, got his bombs
away. Blazing fuel finally engulfed *Eager Eagle*, which hit the
ground, cartwheeled and exploded in flames. Miraculously, two
gunners managed to scramble from the wreckage. McLaughlin
was partially thrown clear of the burning Liberator but he died
in a Romanian hospital two days later. Hughes received a
posthumous Medal of Honor. All five groups received a War
Department Citation for their outstanding performance on the
Ploesti mission of 1 August 1943.

The 389th Bomb Group proudly parade at Hethel with a guidon with a pennant earmarking the raid on Ploesti, 1 August 1943, for which the 'Sky Scorpions' were awarded a Distinguished Unit Citation. (USAF)

During their tour of duty in Europe the 'Sky Scorpions' flew 307 combat missions, dispatching 7,579 successful sorties and dropping over 17,500 tons of bombs, losing 153 B-24s (116 in combat). Gunners were credited with 204 enemy aircraft

389th personnel celebrate Christmas at Hethal. (Russ Hayer)

destroyed. The group flew in nine major campaigns in three zones of operations in the ETO and received a Distinguished Unit Citation and a Medal of Honor for the Ploesti raid. On 24 February 1944 when the 2nd BD set out to bomb the Me 110 assembly plant at Gotha the 239 B-24s were led by the 389th, which lost six B-24s shot down. Some confusion arose at the IP when the 389th lead navigator suffered oxygen failure and veered off course. The lead bombardier slumped over his bombsight and accidentally tripped the bombs but the rest of the group realized the mistake and successfully bombed the target. Intelligence sources estimated that six to seven weeks' production was lost. Four large workshops were destroyed, while several more were damaged though many of the machine tools survived.

On 22 April a mission to the marshalling yards at Hamm was delayed several times because of bad weather at the target. Strong headwinds delayed the approach and caused two groups to miss the yards. The weather and intense flak caused many bombs to go astray. The eleven B-24 groups returned to East

B-24 *Delectable Doris*, the name given to the original Liberator of Bill Graf in honour of his English fiancée, later his wife. (USAF)

Father Gerald Beck, the Catholic chaplain at Hethel, distributes communion to his combat crews after a mission briefing. Driving in his jeep, named *Hellzapoppin*, at top speed, he would go from B-24 to B-24, making sure that no one was denied communion. In North Africa, Father Beck was inside a B-24 administering the sacrament at take-off time and ended up giving Holy Communion in the air during the mission! He flew a number of missions, earning the Air Medal, in order, he claimed, better to understand what the men had to endure, until, eventually, the head chaplain in Europe put a stop to his flying career. Father Beck was probably the most influential driving force behind the men of the 389th Bomb Group. (USAF)

Anglia as darkness descended, unaware that they were being chased by Me 410A-1 *Hornisse* (Hornet) intruders of KG 51 *Edelweiss*, who, led by their CO, Major Dietrich Puttfarken, had taken off from Soesterberg. Holland, to infiltrate the returning bomber stream. The 389th lost two B-24s in the Me 410 attacks.

The 564th Bomb Squadron became a PFF squadron and supplied PFF aircraft to other groups. A 389th Bomb Group crew led the first Liberators over the beaches on D-Day, 6 June 1944. It flew a record four missions on D-Day, launching fifty Liberators, including fourteen pathfinders, some of which were sent to other groups.

Like all US bases Hethel had an officers' club, movie house, gymnasium, library, and other facilities for their use. Occasional dances were held, and women were invited onto the base. Also, a few of the United Services Organization (USO) were held at the base, including celebrities such as Jack Benny, James Cagney

Hethel airfield in April 1946 with Hethel Wood (centre) and Stanfield Hall (top left, below the bomb dump). Paths through Hethel Wood led to naturally concealed billets (right) and the restored chapel building. (DoE)

and Bob Hope. The men played sports; football, baseball, and basketball tournaments were held among the units on the base and with units from other bases. They visited the nearby towns of Wymondham and Norwich. On the occasions when they had a three-day pass, they generally travelled to London.

When on 7 April 1945 the 389th led the 2nd AD to Duneberg, the *Luftwaffe* employed *Rammjäger* fighters (the deliberate ramming of American bombers by converted Bf 109s flown by pilots of *Sonderkommando Elbe*) against American bomber streams. They destroyed seventeen aircraft. One victim was the 389th lead aircraft, *The Palace of Dallas* flown by Lieutenant Bob C. Dallas with the Group Commander, Colonel John Herboth aboard. The Bf 109 bounced off the lead ship, hit the deputy lead ship flown by First Lieutenant Walter K. Kunkel, and this also went down. On 14 April about 122,000 Germans holding out and manning twenty-two gun batteries along the Gironde estuary in the Royan area, which was denying the Allies the use of the port of Bordeaux, were bombed by 1,101 heavies. Five Liberators were hit and *The Bigass Bird* and *Standby* went down. *Is This Trip Necessary?* crash-landed in France and another Liberator limped back to England. The second mission to Royan, on 15 April, was carried out without loss. Nearly 850 heavies of the 2nd and 3rd AD, carrying napalm for the first time, dropped 460,000 gallons in 75–85 gallon liquid-fire tanks on the stubborn defenders of Royan.

Beginning on 3 May Trolley or Revival missions crammed with ground personnel were flown at heights ranging from 1,000 to 3,000 feet over bombed-out German cities. VE (Victory in Europe) Day took place on 8 May. On 20 and 21 May the Liberators finally began leaving Hethel for the Zone of Interior (ZOI) (USA). B-24 *Betty Lee* crashed on 20 May at Manea, Cambridgeshire.

On 25 June 1945 Hethel airfield was transferred to 12 Group, RAF Fighter Command. Flying ceased in late November 1946 and in mid-1947 it became a personnel transit centre. Shortly after, it was transferred to Technical Training Command. It became inactive late in 1948. In March 1952 the pilot of a USAF B-50 Superfortress bomber made a successful forced landing at night on the disused airfield. Running short of fuel, he landed without landing aids or runway lights in darkness and pouring rain. It finished up to the tops of its undercarriage in mud with little damage and the crew unhurt. For a few days afterwards a C-47 Dakota flew in daily with a working party, preparing the B-50 for when it later made a successful take-off.

In November 1966 the Lotus founder, Colin Chapman, moved his road and racing car factory from Cheshunt in Hertfordshire to Hethel. A keen and accomplished pilot, the site offered two particularly attractive features to the dynamic businessman; an airfield for his company aircraft (which he regularly flew himself) and a valuable test track. In addition, Chapman now had a conveniently large site amongst open farmland in which to develop without the cramping regulations of his previous head-quarters. Although the runways were considerably reduced in length due to the adjoining farmer's requirements, the car test track used part of the north-west–south-west main runway and the north-west–south-east runway. A number of the original airfield buildings still remained, which Chapman immediately put to good use also. The former control tower became the Lotus

Sports and Social Club. In the mid-eighties Stuart Main of Lotus Cars set up a small section as a memorial room to the 389th and in 1987 visiting American veterans donated $1,500 for the purchase of display cases to house the memorabilia they had sent him. The former American hospital and its outbuildings sited across Potash Lane leading to the factory entrance, became Factory 6, home to Lotus Racing (1971) and then Team Lotus (1974–7) as well as part of the Chapman boat empire of the seventies. The wartime hangars were in good order after twenty-five years and were similarly utilized for storage etc. In 1984 the supporting frames of the hangars were still in such good condition after forty-two years that they were dismantled, refurbished and the vertical supports cut through, enabling the top 'peaked roof' halves to become the supporting structures for lower buildings, complete with modern insulated wall cladding. The left-over lower halves became similar structures on adjacent sites, thereby doubling the previous factory area.

HORSHAM ST. FAITH (STATION 123)

Built before the war for use by RAF Bomber Command, Horsham St Faith was a grass airfield with five C-type hangars, permanent brick and tiled buildings with central-heating and a high standard of domestic accommodation. The station was officially opened on 1 June 1940 and was used first by Blenheims, and then

The 458th Bomb Group taxi out at Horsham St Faith on Christmas Eve 1944. (USAF)

B-24H 41-28743 *Eastern Beast* of the 785th Bomb Squadron, 466th Bomb Group, at Horsham St Faith. This aircraft crashed at Rivenhall, Essex, on 5 April 1944 after the raid on Siracourt, France. The hangar in the background, which housed the operations, armament, ordnance and engineering sections of the 458th Bomb Group is, like all the others at the airfield, now Norwich Airport, still in use today. (Krause)

The 458th Bomb Group was fortunate to take over pre-war RAF buildings, houses and hangar facilities when they moved into Horsham St Faith in February 1944. A similar situation awaited personnel at other bases in the region, such as Bassingbourn, Duxford, Watton and Wattisham. (Herman Hetzel)

Mosquito light bombers, until the late summer of 1942. In September that year the airfield was transferred to the US 8th AF and although the 2nd Bomb Wing assumed control of the airfield in November 1942 the first American occupants were the 319th Bomb Group (Medium) equipped with B-26 Marauders. The 319th left for North Africa in November 1942 to take part in Operation *Torch*. Then on 5 April 1943 the 56th Fighter Group, equipped with P-47 Thunderbolt fighters, arrived from King's Cliffe in Northamptonshire to fly combat missions. On 12 April administrative control of Horsham St Faith passed from the RAF to Substitution Unit HQ, 2nd Bomb Wing. The wing HQ remained there until 14 September 1943, when it moved to Hethel. Meanwhile, on 8 July 'Zemke's Wolfpack', as the 56th were popularly known, had moved to Halesworth in Suffolk so that work on enlarging Horsham St Faith to accommodate heavy bombers could begin. Three Class A runways and fifty hardstandings were laid and accommodation provided for nearly 3,000 men by building a few dispersed Nissen hut sites to the east of the airfield. Late in January 1944 the 458th Bomb Group arrived.

The Group, which was commanded by Colonel James H. Isbell and was equipped with the latest B-24H and B-24J

Horsham St Faith airfield in April 1946, RAF Mosquitoes and Mustangs can be seen. (DoE)

B-24 *Arise My Love and Come With Me* at Horsham St. Faith. (USAF)

Officers of the 458th Bomb Group in front of the officers' mess and the famous Old Catton 'Cat on the Barrel' village sign at Horsham St Faith. (USAF)

Liberators, was originally activated on 1 July 1943 at Wendover Field, Utah, and had begun assembly on 28 July 1943 at Gowen Field, Idaho. Successively based in Florida, Utah and Nevada the group's training activities came to a close. On New Year's Day 1944 the ground echelon departed by rail from Tenopah, Nevada, for New York, where it embarked on the USS *Florence Nightingale*. The air echelon travelled to Hamilton Field, California, where its new Liberators were waiting to be flown to England. *En route* to the ETO the Liberators took in Brazil and Africa on the southern ferry route. Crews were reunited with the ground echelon at Horsham St Faith on 18 February 1944. First Lieutenant (later Lieutenant General) James M. Keck recalls:

Girls stop to watch as American ground crew attend to a Pratt & Whitney Twin Wasp engine on a Liberator. (USAF)

458th Bomb Group personnel posing for the camera in front of one of the RAF houses in Fifers Lane, Norwich. The houses are still there today. (Herman Hetzel)

Horsham St Faith was a good base – permanent and close to town. We attended church across the street from the club, got fresh eggs for fighter claims (our crew claimed three destroyed, two probables and four damaged – totally unofficial, but it did get us eggs). We hunted birds and rabbits on the airfield and took turns driving the game on bicycles – and had game dinners in our crew mess – courtesy of Dusty Rhodes, our mess sergeant.

On 11 January 1944 Brigadier-General Walter H. Peck and his staff had commandeered part of Horsham St Faith for use as the HQ of 96th Wing. It displaced the 93rd Wing, 3rd BD, which in turn moved its HQ to Elveden Hall, near Thetford, Norfolk.

The 458th flew a diversionary mission on 24 February and made its full operational debut on 2 March when a small formation was

'Sweating' them in. (USAF)

Long queues for the enlisted men's Thanksgiving Dinner, 24 November 1944.(Via Jack Krause)

dispatched to Frankfurt, Germany. PFF equipment was used, flak was moderate and only four Fw 190s were sighted. B-24 42-28669 *Ginny* crashed just after take-off at 9 Pinewood Close, Hellesdon, near the airfield. It had iced up, and partly destroyed the house, killing seven of the crew and a lady in the house and seriously injured the three other crew. The proximity of the airfield to the Norwich suburbs involved some risk to the civilian population and nine more fatal crashes occurred locally during 1944–5.

On 30 May 1944 the 8th AF attempted to bomb bridges at Beaumont-sur-Oise, Melun and Meulan in France. These attacks introduced the revolutionary *Azon* 1,000 pound glider bomb, which could be released by an aircraft at a distance and then directed onto the target using radio-controlled moveable tail fins. General Spaatz had revived interest in the *Azon* after German flak had increased both its area of operation and its effectiveness during the early part of the month, and it fell to the 458th to evaluate the device in combat conditions. Each bomber could carry three such bombs but had to circle the target as many times to release them. Visibility had to be good to enable the operator in the B-24 to keep a visual sighting on it right to the

752nd Bomb Squadron B-24 Liberator in one of the hangars at Horsham St Faith in 1944. (USAF)

On 13 February 1945 B-24J 44-40281 *A Dog's Life* in the 753rd
Bomb Squadron crashed at the junction of Spixworth Road and
Church Street, Old Catton, Norwich, during a training flight
after two engines cut out at 800 feet. All nine crew died and one
woman civilian was injured. (Rick Rockicki)

Liberator of the 753rd Bomb Squadron over Horsham St. Faith.
(USAF)

Returning from a raid on the Herman Göring Works at Halle on Sunday 14 January 1945, B-24J 44-40283 *Lassie Come Home* of the 753rd Bomb Squadron, 458th Bomb Group, with one engine feathered and its landing gear down, crashed upside down in the back garden of 14 Spynke Road, Norwich. All except one of Lieutenant John J. Clayborn's crew were killed and two children playing in the garden also died. (USAF)

The 458th Bomb Group taxi out at Horsham St Faith on Christmas Eve 1944. (USAF)

target. For this purpose a smoke canister was attached. On 30 May four *Azon* Liberators were used and because of the secrecy involved a large force of fighters escorted them. The raid, flown at 10,000 feet, was a failure, with none of the bombs hitting the target. Experimental raids continued into June with at most fifteen Liberators on any one mission. But the results did not improve and prompted General Doolittle, the 8th AF Commanding General, to abandon the project.

On 12 September 1944 the 458th began 'trucking' missions to France, delivering just over 13,000 gallons of fuel to units there. On the 19th twenty-four B-24s of the 458th delivered just over 38,000 gallons to France. Next day, when the missions continued, a 458th Bomb Group Liberator with 1,530 gallons of fuel for the army units crashed in Hastings Avenue, Hellesdon, killing the crew and an occupant of one of the six houses damaged in the explosion. During September, in thirteen days of 'trucking' missions, the 458th delivered 727,180 gallons of fuel to France.

On 24 November 1944 Second Lieutenant Ralph Dooley was returning to Horsham St Faith after a practice mission when his B-24 broke cloud and struck the flagpole on top of the tower of St. Philip's Church in Heigham Street, Norwich. The damaged aircraft crossed Dereham Road at rooftop height. The time was about 1615 hours and it was dusk. Some women in the process of drawing their blackout curtains glimpsed the pilot battling at the controls, bravely trying to gain height and avoid hitting the rows of terraced houses below. Dooley finally put down on waste ground near Barker Street but he and all his crew were killed. Residents of the Heigham Street area later subscribed to a memorial plaque in memory of the crew and it is still displayed near the site of the crash.

Returning from a raid on the Herman Göring Works at Halle on 11 January 1945 B-24 44-40283 *Lassie Come Home* of the 753rd Squadron, with one engine feathered and landing gear down, crashed upside down in the back garden of 14 Spynke Road, Norwich, on approach to Horsham St Faith. All except one of the crew was killed and two children playing in the garden also died. A third child had an incredible escape. On 13 February 1945 B-24J 44-40281 *A Dog's Life* in the 753rd Bomb Squadron crashed at the junction of Spixworth Road and Church Street,

Old Catton, Norwich during a training flight after two engines cut out at 800 feet. All nine crew died and one woman civilian was injured. On 14 April 1945 just after take off B-24H *Hookem Cow* in the 755th Bomb Squadron crashed in the parish of Hainford and *The Bird* in the 752nd Bomb Squadron, crashed at Barrett's farm, Spixworth, killing six men and seriously wounding another.

The 458th Bomb Group remained at Horsham St Faith until mid-1945, flying its 240th and last combat mission on 15 April. It had despatched 5,759 sorties and dropped 13,204 tons of bombs for forty-seven Liberators lost in action and another eighteen to other causes. Horsham St Faith airfield was transferred to RAF Fighter Command on 10 July 1945. It was inactivated in 1963 and the RAF left in 1967. In 1969 Norwich Airport was born and Rig Air (later Air Anglia) began flying scheduled services using DC-3 airliners.

METFIELD (STATION 366)

This airfield was built after the B1123 road running from Halesworth to Harleston was closed, by John Laing & Son Ltd in 1943. Three standard intersecting concrete runways, fifty dispersal points and two T2-type hangars, as well as temporary buildings on farmland to the south-west to accommodate 2,900 men, were built. Though intended as a bomber base the first American arrivals at the airfield in August 1943 were the 353rd Fighter Group, which arrived from the training airfield at Goxhill and were equipped with P-47 Thunderbolts. The group began flying combat missions from Metfield on 12 August and the CO, Lieutenant-Colonel Joseph A. Morris, was lost on 16 August. During its wartime career several 353rd Fighter Group pilots made a name for themselves, foremost among them being Captain Walter Beckham, the top scorer of the 8th AF with eighteen aircraft destroyed at the time of his loss in combat on 22 February 1944. Beckham survived and became a PoW.

Colonel Glenn Duncan, the 353rd CO, reached the conclusion that a squadron, specially trained in the art of ground strafing, would be an ideal weapon and Metfield was selected as the base for the new unit. On 18 March 1944 volunteers from four fighter groups assembled under the command of Colonel Duncan and

Metfield airfield in October 1945. During the war it was the home of the Liberators of the 491st Bomb Group. At the bottom of the photo is the crater left by the bomb dump explosion of 15 July 1944. (DoE)

became the 353rd 'C' Fighter Group at Metfield where a mock target was erected to practise stafing tactics and manoeuvres. The new unit soon became known as 'Bill's Buzz Boys' after General William Kepner who had agreed to establish the unit. However, on 12 April 1944 the 353rd transferred further south to Raydon and Metfield became a heavy bomber airfield again when the B-24 Liberators of the 491st Group arrived on the base.

The group was unusual in that its ground echelon was recruited from personnel at other 2nd BD bases, although 145 key ground personnel, who had left America on 11 April, arrived to supplement the ground echelon. The air echelon, which had taken off from Florida on 1 April, began arriving at Metfield between 18 and 30 May. The group was under pressure to become fully operational by 10 June but its baptism of fire commenced on 2 June when the 95th CBW, whose only other group was the 489th at Halesworth, was given Bretigny airfield near Paris as their target. Lieutenant-Colonel Jack Merrell took his thirty-sixth B-24s from Metfield to rendezvous forty-one Liberators of the 489th. One 491st Bomb Group B-24 was shot down before bombs away but the rest managed to return safely and land in gathering darkness. Missions continued to France and on 4 June. *Sack Rat,* piloted by Second Lieutenant Clifford R. Galley, developed a high-speed stall while forming up and crashed near Sizewell in Suffolk, killing everyone on board.

July 1944 was an unlucky month for the 491st Bomb Group. On the 13th the crash of a B-24 on its approach to Metfield claimed five lives of a replacement crew. Two days later a further tragedy occurred. There was no mission scheduled for that day and during the evening while most of the men were viewing a movie a convoy of trucks carrying bombs was being

During the evening of 15 July 1944 the bomb dump at Metfield, which contained 1,200 tons of high explosive and incendiaries, exploded. The explosion was heard in Great Yarmouth, 25 miles away, where cinema goers thought a V-2 had landed! (Dan Winston)

Aerial view of the area of the Metfield bomb dump explosion.
(USAF)

unloaded at the 476th Sub-Depot at Metfield. There was an
explosion at 7.30 pm and five men were killed. The flaming hulk
of an American army Dodge truck turned and twisted hundreds
of feet into the air before falling to earth three fields away.
Windows were broken in Bungay, 8 miles to the north-east and
the shock wave was felt as far as Southwold, 15 miles away
on the coast. The 3rd SAD maintenance unit was notified of the
blast at 2100 hours. An hour later a UC-64, loaded with
engineering officers, landed at Metfield to survey the damage to
the B-24s. However they returned to Griston because five un-
exploded bombs were scattered about the dispersal area. By
daylight they had been removed and the engineering officers
returned. They found only twenty-nine B-24s operational. Seven
could be repaired at the sub-depot while nine had to be transferred to the 3rd SAD for major repairs and six were salvaged at
Metfield. The 3rd SAD sent several maintenance parties to assist
in the repairs.

Mr Pye, the Chief Foreman of Trades at Metfield recalled:

It seemed the explosion was caused by some engineers who
were unloading bombs from a truck to the bomb dump.

The bombs were not primed and the men were kicking them off the truck and onto the ground. While they were being unloaded in this fashion, one went off starting a chain reaction which destroyed practically the whole store, setting off 1,200 tons of high explosive and incendiaries. The grass from the bomb dump to the hangar was scorched and the bottom of the hangar ripped out. Some time later the truck's differential axle was discovered in a village about a mile from the scene of the explosion, thrown there by the blast!

Less than ½ mile from the centre of the explosion, West End Farm was demolished, luckily without loss of life, and Park Farm to the north was partially damaged. Missions from Metfield were cancelled for three days while HQ held an inquiry. Lieutenant-General James Doolittle, and Major-

Exhausted 491st Bomb Group crew members at Metfield after returning from the group's first combat mission on 2 June 1944.
(USAF)

Briefing for the first mission on 2 June 1944. (USAF)

Generals James P. Hodges and William Kepner headed the investigation, which at first suspected sabotage. An extended loop to the bomb dump was later built to bypass the huge crater, which could still be seen for many years after the war.

In August the 95th CBW was deactivated and the 491st was reassigned to the 14th Wing at North Pickenham in place of the 492nd Bomb Group, which was taken out of combat after suffering heavy losses. The 491st ended the war in April 1945 having flown 187 missions, dropping 12,304 tons of bombs for the loss of forty-seven Liberators in combat and twenty-three non-combat losses.

After the 491st Bomb Group's departure, a small number of Liberators were based at Metfield and the European Division of Air Transport, USSTAF, officially used these. However, while a number of transport aircraft did use the base, the main function was to house a secret unit engaged in clandestine transport operations to Sweden for the purpose of flying out special materials and ferrying personnel. This unit operated from Metfield until the end of the war but used airfields in Scotland as advanced bases. On 4 March 1945 the airfield was strafed by a Ju 88G and one of the occupants of the control tower was killed. Metfield airfield was returned to the RAF in 1945 and subsequently abandoned. The airfield was sold in 1964–5 and the area was returned to agricultural use. St Ives Sand & Gravel and Banham and Sons cleared all the runways and perimeters save for a single-track road. One of the T2 hangars was sold for £2,000 to an east-coast yachting centre and Mr. L. Hadingham of Park Farm bulldozed over the bomb dump crater in 1968–9. The control tower was demolished in 1970.

North Pickenham (Station 143)

This airfield was built to the standard Class A specification, but the main runway was 1,900 yards long and almost all the hard-standings had to be confined to one side of the airfield. The technical site and one of the two T2 hangars were built on the south-east side of the field and accommodation was provided for 3,000 personnel in a valley to the east. The base was originally intended for use by the B-24 Liberators of the 491st Bomb Group, then undergoing training in the USA, but the 492nd was considered to be almost operational so they were selected to occupy the base and join the 14th CBW. The Liberators of the 492nd alighted on the runways at North

North Pickenham airfield in 1946. (USAF)

B-24J 44-40172 *Grease Ball* of the 854th Bomb Squadron, 491st Bomb Group coming in to land. This Liberator was lost over Misburg on 26 November 1944 when 20 mm cannon fire set the bomb bay on fire. Only three of Lieutenant Robert W. Simons's crew escaped. (Dan Winston)

Damage to B-24 44-40124 *Uninvited* of the 853rd Bomb Squadron, 492nd Bomb Group on 15 June 1944. (USAF)

Pickenham in slashing rain on 18 April 1944. Colonel Eugene Snaveley, who landed in *Little Lulu*, had been posted from the 44th Bomb Group at nearby Shipdham to command the 492nd Bomb Group on 26 January 1944. The group flew their first mission on 11 May. On 19 May, when the Liberators went to Brunswick's marshalling yards, the formations were overwhelmed over Holland by over 150 German fighters, and four 492nd Bomb Group B-24s were shot down. A fifth continued to the target but exploded before bombs away. The group lost three more B-24s coming off the rallying point, bringing their total losses to eight – double that of all the other groups combined. Second Lieutenant Wyman Bridges brought *Lucky Lass* home to North Pickenham after a collision with a Bf 109. His aircraft had only two engines and had lost half the starboard wing. His miraculous feat earned him the DFC. The 492nd were stood down the following day. On 27 May a formal ceremony took place on the base to mark the airfield being handed over to the USAAF, the 77th and final British airfield to be allocated to the American Air Force.

On 19 June the 858th Bomb Squadron was transferred on paper to Cheddington, where it became a night leaflet squadron, dropping propaganda material over the Reich. During June and July five crews were transferred to the 44th Bomb Group at Shipdham. On 20 June the 2nd Bomb Divison flew a nine and a half hour round trip to Politz and Ostermoor. Enemy fighters hit the 14th CBW hard over the Baltic; at North Pickenham fourteen Liberators were missing. Lieutenant Velarde's B-24 in the 856th Squadron, which returned early with engine trouble, was the only B-24 from that squadron to make it back. Five, including *Say When*, *Sknappy* and *Silver Witch*, put down at Bulltofta airfield at Malmö in Sweden.

On 7 July the 2nd BD made an eight and a half hour round trip to the Junkers factory at Bernberg and over 200 *Luftwaffe* fighters attacked. The 44th Bomb Group was forced to veer off in order to avoid collision with four other B-24 groups and it took the fighter escort with them leaving the 492nd alone and exposed and eleven B-24s were shot down in quick succession. On 7 August twelve B-24 crews in the 492nd Bomb Group flew its sixty-seventh and final mission from North Pickenham. Losses on the scale of Politz and Bernberg could not continue and the

Wreckage of a 492nd Bomb Group B-24 which crashed in England. (USAF)

B-24J 42-51258 of the 856th Bomb Squadron, 492nd Bomb Group, piloted by Second Lieutenant Karl W. Ruthenbeck, leaves the burning Schulau oil refinery on 6 August 1944. This was the group's penultimate mission and it cost them two B-24s. On 7 August the 492nd flew its 67th and final mission from North Pickenham and then ceased to exist as a combat group. No. 42-51258 joined the 44th Bomb Group in September 1944 and was salvaged on 7 February 1945. (USAF)

492nd officially ceased to exist. It had the highest loss rate of any 8th AF bomb group in the three months it was operational. Between May and August it had lost fifty-one B-24s in combat and six to other causes. Crews and their B-24s were dispersed throughout the 8th AF B-24 groups and the 801st Group (P), Carpetbagger Group, at Harrington received seven of the B-24s and the 492nd's designation. On 10 August 136 officers and 532 enlisted men, late of the 859th Squadron at North Pickenham, were transferred to the 467th Bomb Group at Rackheath to form that Group's 788th Squadron.

On 15 August the 491st Bomb Group at Metfield, which in contrast to the 492nd had lost ten B-24s in the previous three months, was transferred from the 95th CBW, which was disbanded, to North Pickenham to join the 14th Wing. The 491st crews at first would not repaint their B-24 rudders with the black and white wing markings of its predecessor because they feared that the 492nd had been a 'marked' group. The 491st went on to establish the highest rate of combat mission of all B-24 groups and it was awarded a Distinguished Unit Citation for the mission to Misburg on 26 November 1944 when the group lost sixteen out of the thirty-one despatched, all shot down in fifteen minutes. Only the timely intervention of P-51 Mustangs saved the group from total annihilation.

The 491st Bomb Group left North Pickenham in August 1945 and the airfield reverted to an RAF satellite for 258 MU at Shipdham. It was transferred to RAF Bomber Command in March 1948 and became inactive on 26 October that same year. In August 1949 it was transferred back to Maintenance Command and on 12 August 1954, administrative control was assumed by the USAF. Then the airfield reverted to the RAF again and was transferred from Home Command to Bomber Command on 1 December 1958 for the arrival of sixty Douglas Thor intermediate-range surface-to-surface ballistic missiles. The Thor had been adopted for use by twenty squadrons in the RAF in 1957 as Britain's nuclear deterrent until the entry into service of RAF V-bombers carrying nuclear missiles. Each squadron had three missiles, making a total of sixty deployed at bases throughout East Anglia and Yorkshire. The three Thor launch pads were constructed at North Pickenham and Campaign for Nuclear Disarmament staged a major sit-down demonstration outside the site in 1959. In 1963 the Thor missile sites were dismantled because of the vulnerability of fixed positions and the entry into squadron service of the V-bomber force. Hawker Siddeley P.1127/Kestrel F(GA)1 V/STOL aircraft (later the Harrier), which were based at West Raynham from 15 Ocotber 1964 to 30 November 1965, were tested at North Pickenham during 1964 and 1965. It closed in October 1963 and in 1967 the site was sold. In 1988 the Thor missile pads were taken up and the ground returned to farming.

OLD BUCKENHAM (STATION 144)

Taylor-Woodrow Ltd built the airfield in 1942–3 to the standard Class A specification with a main north-east–south-west runway 2,000 yards long and two auxiliary runways each 1,400 yards long joined by a concrete perimeter track with fifty hardstandings. Mark II airfield lighting was available for the main runway.

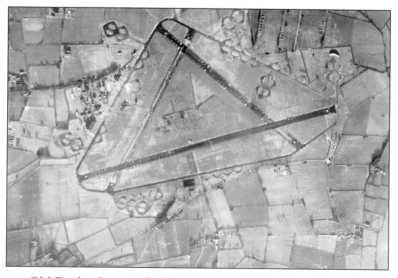

Old Buckenham airfield in January 1947, when obstacles blocked the runways and taxiways. Top left is the mess site with the sick quarters to its right. Below that is the group HQ site and bottom left of that is the communal site. (DoE)

Two T2 hangars were erected, one on each side of the airfield, and accommodation, mostly Nissen huts with a few Maycrete huts, was provided for 2,900 personnel in temporary buildings. The living sites were dispersed in farmland on the western side of the airfield and the bomb store was on the northwestern side. On 22 December B-24 Liberators of the 453rd Bomb Group began flying into Station 144 to form the 2nd CBW's third group in Norfolk.

The 453rd had been activated on 1 June 1943 and Colonel Joseph A. Miller had assumed command soon after. The group continued its training at Pocatello, Idaho, moving to March Field, California, on 30 September. Early in December that year the ground echelon travelled to Camp Kilmer in New Jersey and then to New York to sail to Scotland. Colonel Miller led the air echelon to England on the southern ferry route.

James Stewart sitting on the rail around the top of the control tower at Old Buckenham. (Author)

The group became operational on 5 February 1944 and by 12 April 1945 had flown 259 missions, losing fifty-eight Liberators. The 733rd Bomb Squadron set an unbeaten record of eighty-two consecutive missions without a loss. On 18 March 1944 the CO, Colonel Miller, was shot down by flak over Friedrichshafen flying in a B-24 called *Little Brian*. Some of the crew who baled out were swept across a lake and drowned. Miller survived and was made a PoW. Colonel Ramsey D. Potts succeeded him at Old Buckenham.

On 30 March Major James Maitland Stewart, the Hollywood actor, was assigned to the 453rd Bomb Group as operations officer to replace Major Curtis H. Cofield, who had been killed in action only three days before. Stewart had flown several missions in the 445th Bomb Group at Tibenham, and had led the wing on more than one occasion. He had been awarded the DFC. Over the next few weeks he took his turn as air commander of bombing missions. On 13 April he flew 2nd CBW lead against German aircraft manufacturing installations near Munich. All but one of the 453rd Bomb Group Liberators returned to Old Buckenham. Sergeant Melvin Borne, a ground-crew man in the 733rd Squadron, recalls an occasion when Jimmy Stewart led the wing in *Whiskey Jingles*.

After the mission, when he taxied into the hardstand, I went up on the wing to check how much fuel showed on the sight gauges on the flight deck. I could only get the bottom of the dip stick wet and told Colonel Stewart, 'Sir, you taxied in on fumes.' Well, two days later Stewart led another mission. Refuelling that morning he put a man on each wing tip and we would jump up and down rocking the aircraft and squeezing in about 40 more gallons by rocking all the air pockets out of the fuel cells. Then, before each aircraft taxied on to the runway, we would hand the flight engineer a gas hose up over the back of the wing and he would top off all the mains again until the fuel ran out and over the wing. That night they made it home with about 50 gallons left.

In two months the group led the 2nd BD in bombing accuracy. By now the wiry, highly strung Stewart was 36 years of age, and his combat career was coming to an end. People in high places rightly considered him too valuable to lose and the decision was taken that he would fly no more missions. This really infuriated him. However, he was still on flying status and therefore had to fly a certain number of hours each month to qualify for flight pay. He, therefore elected to fly the 453rd assembly ship, *Wham Bam* during formation for the mission to Bordeaux. Assembly ships were multi-coloured B-24Ds stripped of all armament and used to format the bomb group setting off on a mission. Their task completed, they would return to base, usually after about an hour.

On the mission to Bordeaux, Stewart took off in *Wham Bam* and flew the normal 'racetrack' course around the group's homing beacon, Buncher Six, until the 453rd had formed up. The assembly ship stayed with the group because it identified the group. *Wham Bam* flew on ahead and higher to allow the lead ship to take over. Normally, the assembly ship would then break away and return to base, its task completed. However, on this

B-24D *Wham Bam*. (USAF)

Major James Maitland Stewart, 453rd Bomb Group Operations Officer 30 March–July 1944. Stewart had commanded the 703rd Bomb Squadron, 445th Bomb Group, at Tibenham before joining the 453rd. On 3 June 1944 Stewart was promoted to lieutenant-colonel and on 1 July he moved to 2nd CBW HQ at Ketteringham Hall as Chief of Staff. Stewart was not the only Hollywood star to serve at Old Buckenham; Walter Matthau was an NCO radio instrument fitter on the base. (USAF)

Major James Stewart holding a de-briefing session. (USAF)

particular mission, Stewart pulled out to the left about ¼ mile and stayed there!

Wham Bam flew all the way to the departure point, at Selsey Bill, and by now his crew was getting a little anxious. They thought, 'He'll call in a minute and ask for the course home.' Up came the French coast and the crew thought, 'Surely he'll turn back now', but he did not. He flew in position all the way to Bordeaux and back again with a very excited crew, conscious of the fact that they were flying an unarmed and highly colorful aircraft in a very hostile part of France. They were sworn to secrecy, but Colonel Ramsey D. Potts probably wanted to know where the crew had been for the past six hours! Altogether, Stewart flew twenty combat missions as command pilot, including fourteen wing leads and one division lead. On 3 June 1944 was promoted to lieutenant-colonel and on 1 July he moved to 2nd CBW HQ at Hethel as chief of staff.

Missions in late 1944 culminated on Christmas Eve, with the 453rd playing host to more than 1,250 British children ranging in

A party for 1,250 local children and London Blitz orphans was held at Old Buckenham on Christmas Eve 1944. The British children made toys to donate to 300 French children and B-24J-42-110078 *Liberty Run* of the 735th Bomb Squadron flew the 'Santa Claus Special' to the Red Cross centre at Rainbow Corner in Paris. A cup of coffee was used by an eleven-year-old London girl to christen the B-24, which slipped off the runway during take-off on 25 December, but which took off safely the following morning. *Liberty Run* survived the war and ended her days at Albuquerque, New Mexico. (Jim Kotapish)

age from four to fourteen. They were gathered from the neighbouring villages and towns. Many were orphans or evacuees from the London Blitz. The party had been in the making since 1 November. Some of the personnel conceived the idea of making toys for the children of Paris, so many of whom had never experienced the spirit and thrills of a child's Christmas. The idea spread like wildfire to and among the neighbouring children, who began to donate their own toys or make new ones. Rag dolls, wooden toys and myriads of Christmas cards were enthusiastically donated by these youngsters for their small French allies. Wheels began to grind. The American Red Cross chose more than 300 French children to receive the gifts on Christmas Day at the ARC Club at Rainbow Corner in Paris. The group received permission to fly the gifts to Paris. An all-French speaking crew was chosen to ferry them over. Technical Sergeant Reuben Brockway was chosen to play the part of Santa Claus, uniform and all, but minus the paunch.

A nameless Liberator, veteran of seventy-four missions without an abort, was chosen to act as Santa's reindeer and sleigh. Personnel on the base contributed their PX rations to fill the stockings of the little guests. The Aero Club was all bedecked, even to the Christmas tree. Decorations consisted of silver cones and balls made of chaff. Coloured chains were made of red and silver strips of paper. Lights were added. Everything was set. The children began to arrive in GI trucks and were placed in three groups according to age. Those from four to seven gathered at the Aero Club where they were entertained. Here, too, they received their stockings filled with candies and toys from Santa himself and were served ice-cream and Coke to their heart's content. Those aged seven to eleven were taken out to the perimeter and shown through the planes. Then came the big show.

The procession walked to the hardstand, where a huge

Red Cross girls serving sandwiches at Old Buckenham. (Pat Ramm)

B-24H 41-28654 *Spare Parts* in the 732nd BS on 21 February 1944. (USAF)

Red Cross Girls visit the troops at Old Buckenham. (Pat Ramm)

Lineup of 'meat wagons' at Old Buckenham with B-24 41-28613 *Maid of Fury* of the 733rd Bomb Squadron, 453rd Bomb Group, behind. (USAF)

platform had been erected alongside one of the ships. It was this ship that was to carry the gifts of these youngsters to their little French friends. Judith McDavid, 11-year-old orphan of the Blitz, christened the ship *Liberty Run* with a cup of coffee. Fully loaded, the B-24 attempted to take off but slipped off the runway as the engines were revved up, and take-off was postponed until morning. Meanwhile, those aged eleven to fourteen had been taken to the base theatre, where an amateur magician entertained them. Joined later by those who had witnessed the christening of the plane, the entire group was shown animated cartoons and a comic feature. Then they returned to the Aero Club where they, too, received gifts and filled themselves with candy, ice-cream and cakes. After the last child had been fed, they were returned to their homes. As night fell, the Aero Club was thrown open to all, regardless of rank. Officers and GIs celebrated Christmas Eve in true American style. At the base chapel, Chaplain Healy led the Midnight Mass as many observed Christmas Eve in the ETO as they had observed it at home. Still others celebrated by drowning their sorrows, if they had any, in mild and bitters plus a surprising amount of wine, Scotch and rye. After a final checkup, *Liberty Run* was ready. At 1015 the engines were revved up and the ship raced down the runway and into the air. Two hours and fifteen minutes later, at 1230, it touched down. The precious boxes were eagerly unloaded and disbursed by the Red Cross hostesses and field

A reporter interviews Ray L. Sears (later Lieutenant-Colonel), of the 735th Bomb Squadron (missing in action 29 April 1944) and co-pilot Jim Kotapish from the *Reluctant Dragon* in the 453rd Bomb Group at Old Buckenham, Norfolk, on their return from Berlin on 8 March 1944. (Jim Kotapish Collection)

attendants. At Rainbow Corner in Paris, Santa handed the gifts to the children. Without a doubt *Liberty Run*'s mission was a grand success.

The 453rd was taken off combat operations on 12 April 1945 to prepare for return to the USA and possible redeployment to the Pacific theatre using B-29 Superfortresses. However hostilities in Europe had ceased before the group had time to start its movement, whilst some aircraft and crews had already been transferred to other units remaining in England.

In May 1945, Old Buckenham reverted to Air Ministry control and was used as a satellite for maintenance units until being closed on 20 June 1960. The airfield was sold off between 1960 and 1964, after which extensive demolition took place by St Ives Sand & Gravel during its return to agriculture, much of the hardcore being sold in the Norwich area. Today a single-bay perimeter track remains and one small section of full-width runway. The control tower has been demolished.

RACKHEATH (STATION 145)

Rackheath bomber airfield, on a natural plateau near Sir Edward Stracey's estate, was constructed in late 1942 by John Laing & Son Ltd. The plentiful woodland and general agricultural features were deliberately preserved and helped to camouflage the base. A main runway 2,000 yards long and two others, each 1,400 yards long, were laid. A perimeter track 2.7 miles in length linked all the runways and fifty hardstandings. Two T2 hangars were erected and dispersed living quarters could accommodate 2,900 men in the wooded countryside to the south-west. During construction, 556,000 cubic yards of soil were excavated, 14,000 yards of soakaway drains installed and 504,000 yards of concrete

A wartime view of Rackheath airfield with Salhouse Station (centre right) on the railway line to the right of the airfield. (Allan Healy)

Personnel of 467th Bomb Group on the march at Rackheath.
Colonel Shower, the group CO was a strict disciplinarian and
ordered parades every Saturday morning when possible. In the
background is the technical site. (Allan Healy)

B-24H 41-29375 *Lil Peach* of the 791st Bomb Squadron, 467th
Bomb Group from Rackheath taxis by the control tower at
North Pickenham. (USAF)

laid. A major overhead power line had to be relocated underground to clear the flying approaches. On 31 October 1943 the
ground echelon of the 467th Bomb Group commanded by
Colonel Albert J. Shower left Wendover Field, Utah, and on 27
February 1944 they sailed from New York to Scotland. The air
echelon meanwhile flew the southern ferry route to England,

Men of the 467th Bomb Group performing early-morning
calisthenics in a field at Rackheath airfield on 26 July 1944, all
part of Colonel Albert J. Shower's 'shaping up' programme.
Shower was the only 8th AF group commander to take his
group to England and command it throughout hostilities in
England, bringing the group home to the USA in May 1945.
(Allan Healy)

losing two B-24s in accidents before they arrived at Rackheath.
Colonel Shower remained in command of the group during their
entire stay in East Anglia, a unique achievement, as every other
American group had more than one commander during their
combat tours in England.

Allan Healy, the group's wartime diarist, recorded his
thoughts:

> We were impressed by England's state of siege. The
> wrecked homes and buildings of Norwich showed the
> ruthless hand of the German bombing that we were about
> to return to them a thousand-fold. Every crossroad had its
> tank barriers and pillboxes ready for use. We saw how
> grimly the British citizen was prepared to defend his home-

B-24H 42-52534 *Witchcraft* (right) of the 790th Bomb Squadron, 467th Bomb Group, undergoing an engine change at its dispersal area at Rackheath. This most famous of all Liberators never had to abort a mission through mechanical failure. (Allan Healy)

land . . . We were based in Norfolk, inland of that great bulge on the East coast of England directly across the North Sea from Holland – the nearest bomber base to Germany and the hostile shore . . . Rackheath was the name of the

B-24 *Screw Ball* in the 467th BG. (Allan Healy)

Loading bombs at the Rackheath bomb dump. (Allan Healy)

park and small village of the estate of Sir Edward Stracey, Bart. His large, Georgian house stood in the center of the park at the end of a long drive coming in from the Norwich–Wroxham road. The gateway to this drive was a beautiful set of gates brought from Paris and called the Golden Gate. Some of his farms, with thatched cottages and open straw stacks, intermingled with the Nissen huts we used, spotted about in clusters under his tall beeches and chestnuts. Other of the farms and their woods and hedgerows had been levelled for our runways. The air base was completely mingled with farm, field and spinney. Pheasants crowed near the barrack sites and rabbits came out in the late evenings about the Operations Block. It was a lovely spot, even to homesick Americans . . . The Air Ministry had built our base. Its plan was far different from that of American bases. There were no serried rows of bleak buildings with grass and trees scraped from the ground and everything barren, efficient, and a scar on the landscape. Rackheath had benefited from the necessities of camouflage. Nissen huts were grouped under tall trees at the edge of woods and in and under them. Roads passed under rows of fruit trees. The farm croft and byre were left untouched. One site was far down by the rhododendron drive, another across the Jersey pasture where the ornamental sheep and tame deer grazed. You walked through a bluebell-carpeted wood in spring from Site 1 to the Operations Block, and past straw ricks from there to the Briefing Building. A hedgerow lined the lane of a civilian-travelled road right through the base, where, on Sundays, the children stood and asked, 'Any gum, chum?' Much of the farm-like quality of the countryside was preserved so that from the air only the slash of the runways showed.

The *Luftwaffe* had about given up bombing when we arrived. But our first days had alerts. We heard the uneven droning of German planes and went out to look. Some few went to the shelters. The searchlights all about us stabbed the sky and we heard the crack of anti-aircraft fire. On the first two raids, shell fragments fell on our base. It was not long, however, before the Tannoy call of 'Enemy aircraft in area' or even 'Enemy aircraft overhead' only awakened us to roll over in our sacks. Each felt a tightening of the stomach, nevertheless, and began to think of the reality of warfare. Many of these nights we heard the RAF going out – a loud hum and roar that filled the sky and went on incredibly long . . . Splasher 5 at Cromer was the familiar place of assembly and return. Great Yarmouth and Lowestoft were our front doors on the North Sea. Beachy Head, Dungeness, Orfordness, Spithead, all became the familiar points from which we would depart for the enemy coast.

Ronald D. Spencer, an airman at Rackheath, recalls:

Home for the bomber crew officer personnel in our squadron was a Nissen hut accommodating twelve crew-members or four crews, each consisting of a pilot, co-pilot, and navigator. The hut was small, approximately 20 by 30 feet, with a concrete floor and the typical corrugated steel hemispherical construction. A small vestibule with double doors (for blackout protection) was supposedly located at one end. A single door provided access at the other end. Warmth in cold weather (which it usually was) was supposedly provided by a small stove located in the centre. Government issue fuel consisted of large chunks of coal, actually coke. We quickly found that you could consume the whole weekly allotment of 52 pounds of coke in one day if you wanted to keep the hut comfortable. During the really cold weather, everyone requisitioned (stole) extra blankets in an effort to keep warm. At one time I had nine.

Ralph Elliott, a pilot in the group adds:

The huts were lined but not insulated so were pretty cold in the wintertime. Rats would get in between the lining and when things got dull we'd chase them out to shoot at with our .45s – never hit any. We had a coke burner in the middle of the room and when it was going the ones near it cooked while the ones at the ends froze – when we had fuel that is.

The 467th Bomb Group, known affectionately as the 'Rackheath Aggies', flew 212 combat missions starting with the first on 10 April 1944, losing twenty-nine Liberators in action. Three weeks later, on 22 April, German intruders attacked airfields in Norfolk and Suffolk, including Rackheath. An Me 410 made a pass over the airfield at 50 feet, firing tracers and dropping two bombs. A Liberator which was undergoing repairs under floodlights at the southern end of the airfield was hit and Joe Ramirez, crew chief of *Witchcraft*, standing only one dispersal away, saw Private Daniel F. Miney killed as he cycled across the concrete. Private Michael F. Mahoney, a ground crewman working on the B-24 under floodlights was wounded in the explosion. The other burst destroyed a cottage in the vicinity. Two of the group's B-24s were lost. First Lieutenant Stalie C. Reid's Liberator in the 791st Squadron went down at Barsham. Seven of the crew perished, trapped in the burning bomber.Second Lieutenant James A. Roden's B-24 in the 788th Squadron crashed at Mendham with the loss of two crew.

From 19 September to 3 October 1944, when the 96th Bomb Wing flew no combat missions, the three groups ferried petrol for General Patton's tanks and motorized units in France. During its fourteen days of 'trucking' the 467th delivered 646,079 gallons of 80-octane fuel to the Allied armies, first to Orleans-Bricy airfield south of Paris and later to Clastres near Saint-Quentin and Saint Dizier.

The German thrust into the Ardennes in December 1944 during a period of bad weather that grounded the Allied air forces caught the American units cold and a salient was opened up in the American lines. It was not until Christmas Eve that the fog lifted sufficiently for the 8th AF to mount its long awaited strike. Traces of overcast still hung in the air as every available Liberator and Fortress crew got airborne from East Anglia for a maximum effort aimed at relieving pressure on the troops trapped in the 'Bulge'. A record 2,034 bombers, including war-weary hacks, and even assembly ships, contributed to this, the largest single strike flown by the Allied air forces of the war. At Rackheath a record sixty-one Liberators, including the assembly ship, *Pete the POM Inspector*, armed only with carbines in the waist positions, were airborne in only thirty minutes. A follow-up raid was ordered for Christmas Day. Two of the 467th Bomb Group's B-24s were shot down by German fighters and a third, *Bold Venture III*, flew on after taking hits in one engine which caused it to catch fire. The crew baled out after the navigator and bombardier had put the aircraft on automatic pilot. The empty

Bicycle check at Rackheath. (Allan Healy)

B-24H 41-29385 *Double Trouble* at Rackheath. (Allan Healy)

Liberator flew on to Wales where, out of fuel, it made a perfect bellylanding in a Welsh marsh!

The bad weather persisted, severely restricting operations on 26 December. The situation in the Ardennes was so desperate that despite bad weather on 29 December 8th AF HQ decided that a strike must go ahead. At Rackheath a ground fog came in over the base at take-off time and reduced visibility to a few feet. Colonel Shower decided to let the lead and deputy lead aircraft from each squadron take-off. These six aircraft would take off on instruments and climb to form a skeleton formation and then fire flares. As the others came up it was hoped that they would spot the flares and take up a prearranged position in the formation. The visibility was so bad that pilots had difficulty in seeing the edge of the runway in the freezing fog. Tommy Dungar, fifteen at the time, recalls:

> We were unloading timber from the rail trucks at Wroxham station yard and everything was so still and covered with white, raw frost and sound carried that morning. We heard the first B-24 start its take-off and the noise of the engines got louder than normal and in the end they were whining and seemed to be pushed far beyond their safety limits. As

it passed over us it was much lower than normal take-offs with white and purple flashes coming from the exhausts. We could barely see the numbers on the nose, as it seemed to part the swirling fog. It had only just made it and must have been very low indeed as it passed over the first houses in Wroxham. [Colonel Al Wallace, CO of the 791st Bomb Squadron, made it – just. The crew evacuated the B-24 after heading the plane out to sea.] As the next B-24's engines got louder, there was a sharp crack like large branches of a tree breaking off, followed by a loud bump. [The tail section and part of the waist area of the B-24 broke off as it hit the trees. A gunner survived and staggered along the rail line and back to the base.] This was followed by sets of small explosions as flares and ammo went off. [The second B-24, deputy lead of the 791st Bomb Squadron, made a wheels-up landing in a field.] We could hear the engines of another B-24 starting its take-off and at the same time there was about six to eight loud explosions all in a matter of seconds. At the same time there was a single and deafening explosion that seemed to be in the air and at almost the same time a lot of thuds and crunching sounds. [The third B-24 had touched a tree on take-off and crash-landed minutes later at Attlebridge.] *Topper II* exploded in the air as it passed over the crashed B-24 [deputy lead of the 791st Bomb Squadron] as its bombs exploded. *Topper II* was blown to pieces in the air and the wreckage fell almost on top of the crashed B-24.

In all, 15 aircrew were killed and four injured.

During the last few months of the war the 'Rackheath Aggies' led the 8th AF in bombing accuracy. *Witchcraft* set a record too, flying 100 missions, all without once turning back, the first on 10 April 1944 and the 100th on 14 January 1945. On 14 April the 8th bombed a pocket of German resistance holding out in the Royan area of France at Point de Grave and twenty-four B-24s of the 467th dropped all their 2,000 pound bombs within 1,000 feet of the MPI, half the bombs falling within a 500 foot circle. This was a bombing pattern unsurpassed in 8th AF history. Next day the 467th and other B-24 groups dropped 460,000 gallons of napalm on the position.

VE (Victory in Europe) Day took place on 8 May. Five days

B-24J 42-110107 in the 467th Bomb Group takes a direct hit in
the wing tanks over the target at Oschersleben on 29 June 1944.
The pilot, Lt. William H. Counts, who was blown out of the
aircraft, was the only survivor. (USAF)

later a Victory Flypast was made over Widewing, the 8th AF
HQ, where Lieutenant-General James H. Doolittle and his staff
were housed. The 467th was given the honour of leading the
formation of about 1,400 bombers and fighters with Colonel
Albert Shower in the leading B-24, but while the heavies were on
course to High Wycombe clouds moved in. Bad weather forced
the formation of B-24s and B-17s down under the cloud layer
and they followed the usual formation landing procedure to get
back on the ground. Final honours therefore went to more than
700 American fighters.

The 467th returned to the USA and on 15 July 1945 Rackheath
was taken over by 42 Group RAF and became 94 Maintenance
Sub-Unit (MSU), responsible for the storage and maintenance of
explosive stores. In 1959 94 MSU left Rackheath and the technical site was later adapted for use by light industry with
numerous new buildings added in recent years. The control
tower which stood derelict after being used as an office for a car
breakers yard for many years is gradually being returned to its
former glory.

SEETHING (STATION 146)

Built in 1942–3 by main contractors John Laing & Son Ltd. Seething had the standard Class A requirement for heavy bombers with a main south-west–north-east runway 2,000 yards long and two 1,400-yard long runways running north-west–south-east and west-east, encircled by a perimeter track 3 miles long. There were fifty-one hardstandings comprising seventeen loops and thirty-four frying-pan type and two T2 hangars on the northern and southern boundaries. Temporary buildings to the south-east of the airfield could accommodate 2,900 men. Before building work was completed in the autumn of 1943, Wellington, X3882 of 29 Operational Training Unit (OTU), attempted a landing on 28 April 1943. It crashed through building materials at the front of Thwaite Cottages and was wrecked. During November and December 1943 the 448th Bombardment Group, commanded by Colonel James N. Thompson, with B-24 Liberator bombers arrived at Seething and was part of the 20th CBW which also included the 93rd at Hardwick and the 446th at Bungay. Colonel Thompson was killed on 1 April 1944, his successor being Colonel Gerry L. Mason. During their stay at Seething the group flew a total of

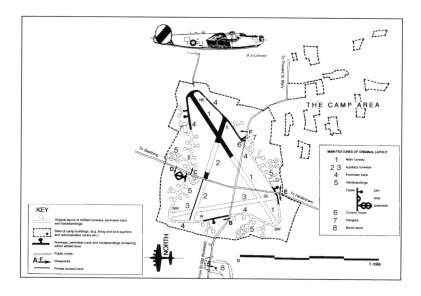

A wartime view of Seething airfield. (via Dugger)

262 missions, dispatching 7,343 sorties, dropping 13,286 tons of bombs and claiming forty-seven enemy aircraft destroyed with total losses of 135 aircraft (101 in action). The 448th flew their first combat mission on 22 December 1943 and the last on 25 April 1945. The assembly ship, B-24D 41-23809, was painted in a black and yellow checkerboard pattern overall and known to some of the locals as 'Old Checky'.

On 31 March 1944 an Me 410 circled the area for over an hour, strafing the perimeter with 20 mm shells. On 22 April 1944, as the B-24s returned in darkness from an attack on Hamm, six Me 410 intruders stalked them as they reached the Suffolk coast. In the 448th 41-28843 and 42-94744 *Peggy Jo* were shot down and fell at Kessingland and on the railway line at Worlingham respectively. Aircraft 42-73497 *Vadie Raye* of the 713th Bomb Squadron was set ablaze, as the pilot, Lieutenant Alvin Skaggs reported.

448th BG using a fighter drop-tank for sailing on the Norfolk Broads. (Author)

American Red Cross minstrels show at Seething. (Newton L. McLaughlin)

As we approached the downwind leg with the base just off to our left an Me. 110 [sic] made a pass at us and riddled our mid-section with hard-nose, soft-nose and 0.30 calibre tracer bullets. From my vantage I barely got a glimpse of him as he came from behind and passed across to our left. Later I learned that ground defences shot this one down. He had made his pass from our right rear, crossing us at about a 40-degree angle. His tracers cut some of our fuel and started a fire in the bomb bay section.

The fire swept from the rear of the bomb bay to the mid-section. By now three of the crew had baled out. Skaggs remained to try to bring the B-24 in safely.

Vadie Raye was now too low for any of the crew in the cockpit and forward section to bale out so my only, alternatives were either to reach a safe altitude for baling out or try to reach the field for a landing. All too soon the engines stopped running. I glanced back at the fire in the bomb bay and could see Master Sergeant George Glevanik standing on the catwalk over the bomb-bay doors right next to the flaming fuel lines. Seconds later the two outside engines suddenly sprang to life and I was able to climb back to pattern altitude of 1,000 feet. I later learned that George was able to get some fuel to the engines by holding his bare hands very tightly over the breaks in the lines.

Skaggs was able to bring the burning Liberator down to the runway at Seething. While it was rolling at 70–80 mph

At work in the Officers' Mess at Seething. (USAF)

On 22 April 1944 the 2nd BD were sent off late in the day to bomb the marshalling yards at Hamm, Germany. The return, in darkness, was shadowed by Me 410s of KG51, which shot down several B-24s in their circuits and generally caused mayhem over the bases. One of the worst hit was the 448th Bomb Group base at Seething, where five Liberators crashed at the end of the runway. In this photograph, B-24H 41-28595 *Ice Cold Katie* lies between B-24H 41-29240 *Tondelayo*, flown by Lieutenant J. L. Barak and on the right B-24H 41-9575 *The Ruth* E. K. Allah Hassid. In all, thirteen Liberators crashed or crash-landed in east Norfolk on the night of 22 April. Two more were damaged on the ground. Over sixty men were killed and twenty-three injured. The fires at Seething were not extinguished until 0330 hours the following morning. (via Francis X. Sheehan)

the navigator and two others went up through the top hatch and rolled out over the wing. Miraculously they all survived. Skaggs and the others scrambled from the wreckage. Glevanik was the last to extricate himself. Altogether, five 448th Bomb Group Liberators crashed at the end of the runway. In all, thirteen Liberators crashed or crash-landed in east Norfolk on the night of 22 April. Two more were damaged on the ground. Over sixty men were killed and another twenty-three injured. The fires at

Seething were not extinguished until 0330 hours the following morning.

The 448th left for the USA in June 1945. On 6 July Seething was transferred to the RAF. On 15 July 1945 42 Group took over and Seething became a sub-site for 53 MU, Pulham, becoming a storage and breaking unit for bombs and armaments. The bombs were stored on the runways and armaments, including hand grenades, in buildings. The airfield was later used by 200 MU until it disbanded in July 1956. In the 1950s some of the barracks near Ivy Farm were used as council living accommodation.

In 1960 five enthusiasts formed the Waveney Flying Group at Seething. During the summer months the runways and peri-track on the eastern side of the airfield were put back into use and although the new Seething–Hedingham road ran across the middle of the airfield, club aircraft like the Tiger Moth and Miles Messenger could use all three runways. The two T2 hangars had been removed but most of the other buildings remained, including the airfield defence gun pits. During the winter a hangar of 2,000 square feet was erected by members, which can accommodate three aircraft. By 1961 the Waveney Flying Group

The less-than-inhibited Americans on the air bases marked VE Day with memorable celebrations, which surpassed even the wildest Fourth of July parties. Here, flares are being fired off at Seething. (via Pat Everson)

Children's' Christmas party at Seething. (via Pat Everson)

had over sixty full flying members. The caravan club house had been replaced by a prefab building with a licensed bar, telephone, mains water and toilets. By 1971 a new road cut across the airfield from Woodton to Thwaite, The licensed runway 07/25 was 665 yards long with a section at the west end unlicensed 283 yards long.

On 22 August 1971 at the annual air show, renowned veteran pilot Neville Browning, who began his flying in the First World War, crashed while flying inverted in his Zlin-Trener-Master G-ASIM and was killed. He had appeared in the film *633 Squadron* and in the pre-title sequence he is seen picking up an agent from the Continent in his own Messenger, filmed in a field near Elstree. Early in 1976 Seething was used by the BBC as a location for a jungle airstrip scene involving a Dakota for the TV series about the life of Orde Wingate. The control tower was painted with a peculiar patchwork camouflage scheme and wooded areas to the south served as the Burmese jungle. Today Seething airfield boasts a thriving aero club and a control tower museum.

The Eightballs taxi out at Shipdham. (USAF)

SHIPDHAM (STATION 115)

The first US heavy bomber base in Norfolk, Shipdham was also continuous host to B-24 Liberators longer than any other 8th AF airfield in Britain – from October 1942 to June 1945. It was built in 1941–2 at a total cost of £1,100,000 to the standard Air Ministry design for bomber fields with three intersecting runways, encircling taxiway and thirty aircraft dispersal points, all concrete with macadam surfacing. Three T2 hangars were grouped together adjacent to the technical site buildings on the south side of the field and the camp was dispersed among fields and farms to the south-east. When the base was allocated to the USAAF, twenty-five additional hardstandings were constructed. The total area of concrete laid was 550,000 square yards; accommodation was constructed for 460 officers and 2,660 enlisted men and petrol storage for 216,000 gallons.

The base opened in September 1942 and was first occupied by personnel of the 319th Bomb Group, which had arrived in Britain on the *Queen Mary* and awaited the arrival of their B-26 Marauders from the USA. However, they moved early in October to Horsham St Faith without receiving their aircraft, Shipdham now awaited the arrival of the 44th Bomb Group and its B-24D Liberators. The 44th, or the the 'Flying Eightballs' as they were known, arrived on 10 October. Although this was the first group to be equipped with the Liberator it had been held back in the USA while it helped form other B-24 groups. The group was initially under strength, as one of its three squadrons

Two aerial views of the technical site and runways at Shipdham airfield in June 1997. (Author)

had been detached in the USA, and not until March 1943 was the 506th Squadron sent to rectify the situation.

On 7 November 1942 the 'Eightballs' flew their first mission of the war when eight B-24Ds, each displaying 'Flying Eightball' emblems, flew a diversionary sweep for B-17s attacking positions in Holland. Two days later twelve B-24s of the 44th and 93rd went to St Nazaire in France to bomb the submarine pens. Thirty-five B-17s went in first followed by the B-24s. All flew at 500 feet to avoid enemy radar, before climbing to heights

On 15 February 1943 twenty-one 44th Bomb Group B-24D Liberators attacked Dunkirk but failed to hit their target, the *Togo*, a German fighter-control ship. The lead aircraft, B-24D 41-23783 *Betty Anne*, piloted by Captain Art V. Cullen with Major Donald MacDonald, 67th Squadron CO, was hit by flak and a huge explosion scattered debris among the formation, hitting another Liberator, whose pilot managed to recross the Channel and force-land at Sandwich. MacDonald died later in a German hospital and Cullen, who was captured, was repatriated in September 1944. (USAF)

Sack Artists in the 67th BS at Shipdham. (USAF)

ranging from 7,500 to 18,000 feet to bomb the target. The Fortresses suffered losses but the Liberators, bombing from 18,000 feet, came through intact.

When the 93rd was transferred to North Africa to assist in operations from December 1942 until February 1943, the 44th flew separate diversionary sweeps for the B-17 Groups. So many of these diversions were flown that the Liberator crews began to call themselves the 'Second Bombardment Diversion'. The problem caused by the differing performance of the Liberators and the Fortresses was highlighted again on 3 January 1943 when the target was again St Nazaire. Eight B-24Ds of the 44th flying in the rear accompanied sixty-eight B-17s to the submarine pens. By the time the formation had reached the target the Liberators had caught up with the B-17s and were able to bomb at higher altitude. It was on this occasion that the 8th abandoned individual bombing in favour of group bombing. The Liberators bombed through the Fortress formations and the practice continued on other missions to the submarine pens.

In July 1943 the 'Eightballs' (and the 93rd and 389th) flew to Libya in North Africa for missions in support of the Italian campaign. Then, on 1 August, the three groups took part in the

low-level mission to Ploesti. Colonel Leon Johnson (left), the CO, led thirty-seven B-24s in the bombing of the Columbia Aquilla and Creditul Minier Brazi refineries. Leon Johnson was awarded the Medal of Honor for his leadership and he received the award at a ceremony at Shipdham on 23 November 1944.

Many Allied bombers made emergency landings at Shipdham. The most famous was on the night of 3/4 November 1943 when RAF Bomber Command raided Düsseldorf. Acting Flight Lieutenant William 'Bill' Reid RAFVR of 61 Squadron in 5 Group and his seven man crew of Lancaster Mk III LM360 O-Oboe were attacked *en route* by a

Major-General George E. Stratemeyer stops to talk with Colonel Leon Johnson, CO, 44th Bomb Group, Major Howard 'Pappy' Moore, and Lieutenant Robert I. Brown by the nose of B-24D 41-23817 *Suzy Q* of the 67th Bomb Squadron at Shipdham on 21 April 1943. In the background is B-24D 41-24278 *Miss Dolores*, which was lost in the North Sea after bombing Kiel on 14 May 1943. (USAF)

twin-engined night fighter shortly after crossing the Dutch coast. Reid's windscreen was shattered by fire, the rear turret was badly damaged, the communications system and the compasses were put out of action and the elevator trimming tabs of the Lancaster were damaged. The bomber became difficult to control. Reid was wounded in the head, shoulders and hands. Despite his wounds and damage to the aircraft, he carried on to Düsseldorf but *O-Oboe* was attacked again, this time by an Fw 190. The German raked the Lancaster from nose to tail with

44th BG personnel playing volleyball at Shipdham and riding the country lanes near the base. (Bill Cameron)

cannon fire, injuring and killing members of the crew and putting out the oxygen system, but still Reid pressed on. He flew the course to and from the target by the Pole Star and the moon. He was growing weak from loss of blood and the emergency oxygen supply had given out. With the windscreen shattered the cold was intense and he occasionally lapsed into semi-consciousness. Despite the odds, however, he and his crew returned to England. He landed at Shipdham, where ground mist partially obscured the runway lights and Reid was also much troubled by blood from his head wound getting into his eyes. With the hydraulics shot out, he had no brakes for landing and the legs of the damaged undercarriage collapsed when the load came on but he got *O-Oboe* down safely. The Lancaster skidded to a halt on its belly as ambulances and crash wagons raced over to the unexpected arrival to help get everybody out of the plane. Reid was given a blood transfusion and spent four days at the Norfolk and Norwich Hospital, before being transferred to a military hospital. While convalescing that he was told he had been awarded the VC. The citation reads:

Wounded in two attacks, without oxygen, suffering severely from cold, his navigator dead, his wireless operator fatally wounded, his aircraft crippled and defenceless, Flight Lieutenant Reid showed superb courage and leadership in penetrating a further 200 miles into enemy territory to attack one of the most strongly defended targets in Germany. Every additional mile increased the hazards of the long and perilous journey home. His tenacity and devotion to duty were beyond praise.

That same night the crew of Halifax B.II HX179 ZA-L of 10 Squadron, flown by Pilot Officer Robert Cameron, was apparently forced to turn back, possibly after being hit by flak or fighters, or with engine trouble, and it too made an emergency landing at Shipdham. As he descended

'Sweating' them in. (Bill Cameron)

B-24D 42-72858 *Pistol Packin' Mama* lifts off from Shipdham. On 9 April 1944 Lieutenant Hiram C. Palmer was forced to land *Pistol Packin' Mama* at Bulltofta, Sweden, after sustaining damage on the Berlin-Marienburg mission. All ten crew were interned. The 'Eightballs'' assembly aircraft, B-24D 41-23699 *Lemon Drop*, a veteran of the Ploesti mission of 1 August 1943, can be seen in front of the hangar. (Bill Robertie)

Shipdham airfield showing the 'stave and crotchet' design of the hardstandings off the peri track. Bottom right is the technical site and bottom left is the bomb dump, stretching into the grounds of Letton Hall. Some conversion work from frying pan to spectacle type dispersals can be seen. (USAF)

the Halifax struck telephone lines and crashed, bursting into flames, at 2115 hours on land farmed by the Patterson family. Cameron and five of his crew all perished in the fire. Ernie Bowman, a member of the Home Guard, was sitting with his wife and their newborn child as the Halifax crashed 60 yards from his home. Ernie could see the flames but noticed that the

Control tower and hangars at Shipdham. (Bill Cameron)

44th BG Christmas card with fake snow and B-24 Southern Comfort. (USAF)

In the control tower at Shipdham. (USAF)

rear of the bomber was not alight and tried to get Sergeant Jack Winstanly, who was unconscious, out of the rear turret. The latter's parachute was snagged and Ernie had to rush home and get a knife. On the way he met his brother-in-law, Sergeant William Wilkins of Norfolk Police, hiding behind a tree that earlier Ernie had sheltered behind for safety, and they returned to the aircraft. The two men removed Winstanly's parachute and got him out onto the ground. However, he died of his injuries in hospital two days later. Ernie Bowman was awarded the British Empire Medal and two American servicemen were awarded the Soldiers' Medal for the rescue.

The 44th flew a total of 343 missions, the last on 25 April 1945. Its gunners were credited with 330 enemy fighters shot down and its own losses, highest of any B-24 group in the 8th, were 153.

During 1946 and 1947 Shipdham became a transit centre for German PoWs *en route* from Florida for repatriation to Germany. Part of the airfield was sold in 1957 and the remainder in 1962 and 1963. In the late 1960s, Arrow Air Services acquired the airfield from a local farmer, Mr. E. A. Savory, and in September 1969 planning permission was received to reopen the airfield. In April 1970 work began on the erection of a new 120 by 95 foot hangar, reception area, workshop and stores etc. Two of the concrete runways were refurbished, together with the approach road and perimeter track. The runway lights were found to be still service-able although they had to be brought up to 1970 standards. In all, the work was completed in a record 14½ weeks. The airfield opened on 16 June 1970, operating initially a Mooney Super 21 and Twin Comanche G-AXRW, which crashed into the trees on the northern boundary of the airfield on 23 January 1973, killing five of the six occupants. Another crash occurred on 1 July 1974 when a Piper Cherokee (G-ATNB) hit a caravan on a taxiway.

Since the war many American veterans have made a pilgrimage back to their old airfields. Forrest S. Clark, a B-24 gunner in the 44th Bomb Group recalls:

> A Norfolk native who frequents the old airfields in the region told me that on moonlit nights one can drive around the abandoned perimeter tracks of the airfields and feel the presence of those who have gone before, the airplanes and the men. He said it always happens as when one of the bombers was lost, a mysterious quiet descends on the scene and there's no sound not even that of the night birds singing. Ghosts haunt those areas and the runway. I know because I have felt them and they do not let one pass without making themselves known. When I stand on an old abandoned runway or control tower and look out across

the old base I hear many sounds, engines warming up, the roar of take-offs, the squeal of landing wheels as they hit the runway after a long mission, and that peculiar squeaking sound and the whisper as the engines were cut off and the bomber came to rest. However, above all these sounds there are the faint words of a song that comes back on the slight wind across the English fields like a whisper from our youth, summoning the past. We would be coming back from a mission, tired, disgusted, many times ill from the cold and high-altitude flying. Suddenly, over the intercom, silent on most returns from a mission we would hear a voice singing, 'Roll me over, Roll me over, Lay me down and do it again.' It's the voice of our navigator, Lieutenant Robert Weatherwax, his flight cap pushed far back on his forehead.

TIBENHAM (STATION 124)

This airfield, alternatively known as Tivetshall, a village in which part of the base was located, was constructed during 1941–2 on the site of what was a First World War Class 3 military landing ground covering 30 acres. In 1916–17 it was used by detachments of 51 Squadron and in 1918 by 75 Squadron. Both squadrons were used on home-defence duties including anti-Zeppelin patrols, flying Avro 504, BE2., Sopwith Pup and Bristol F2b fighters. In 1941 work began on the construction of a bomber airfield and the main contractor was W. & C. French Ltd. The standard 2,000-yard-long main south-west–north-east and two runways each 1,400 yards long running north-west–south-east and west-east were laid. Branching off the perimeter track were thirty-six frying-pan type hardstandings and sixteen loops. Two T2 hangars were built, one on the south side and one on the eastern side of the airfield and dispersed sites were constructed in the farmlands on the eastern side to house 2,900 men.

The airfield was turned over to the USAAF in November 1942 when personnel of two B-26 squadrons of the 320th Bomb Group stayed for just a few days before going to North Africa. During the summer of 1943 Tibenham was assigned to the 2nd Bomb Wing (later the 2nd Bomb Division) and was used by a few B-24

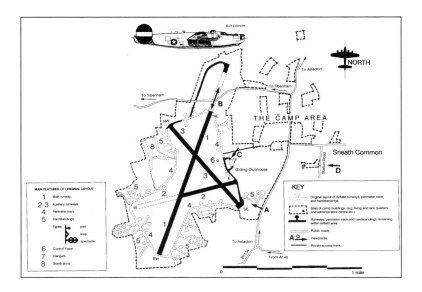

Tibenham airfield in April 1946 showing the village of
Tibenham (top left) and Tivetshall (bottom right). The main
living sites are in the parish of Aslacton (top right). (USAF)

James Maitland Stewart, born of Scottish-Irish parents on 20 May 1908 in Indiana, Pennsylvania, where his father was a hardware merchant, studied architecture at Princeton University, New Jersey, where he acted while a student. By 1940 he had appeared in over twenty movies and won an Academy Award for his role in *The Philadelphia Story*. In 1941 Stewart enlisted in the AAC (he owned his own aircraft, had logged over 200 hours of civilian flying and possessed a commercial pilot's licence). In January 1942 he received his commission and 'wings' and on 7 July 1942 was promoted First Lieutenant. Finally in August 1943 he was posted to the 445th Bomb Group at Sioux City, Iowa, as Operations Officer of the 703rd Bomb Squadron. In November 1943 the 445th left for Tibenham, Suffolk, on the southern ferry route and he flew over with the crew of *Tenovus* (pictured kneeling, far left, at Marrakech, Morocco, *en route*). (James N. Kidder via Pat Ramm)

training aircraft but it was not until November that the 445th Bomb Group, flying B-24 Liberators, arrived to take up permanent station. This group had been activated at Gowen Field, Idaho, and during early June 1943 moved to the salt flats at Wendover Field, Utah. From August until September three crashes occurred during training flights killing twenty-seven airmen and crews became unsettled, claiming that they were a jinxed group.

In October sixty-two crews were ready to fly the southern ferry route to England and one of the B-24s was lost *en route*. On 6 November the 445th assumed complete administrative control of Tibenham from the RAF and officers from Wing HQ at Hethel constantly checked on the group's progress. The 445th flew its first mission on 13 December 1943. In February 1944 an un-

James Stewart at Tibenham (Tibenham Gliding Club)

fortunate incident occurred at Tibenham when bad weather conditions caused a 2nd Division Liberator to jettison a bomb whilst flying over the airfield killing two airmen and a woman in a nearby house.

James Maitland Stewart, the famous Hollywood actor, served in the 445th Bomb Group, first as Operations Officer and then Commanding Officer of the 703rd Bomb Squadron. He flew about twenty combat missions in B-24s, including fourteen wing leads and one division lead. His first mission was on 13 December 1943, when he led the high squadron to bomb the naval docks at Kiel. On a mission to Bremen three days later and one to Calais on Christmas Eve, Stewart showed his mettle, demonstrating a high degree of training and leadership ability. On 7 January 1944 420 B-17s and B-24s caused considerable damage to the I. G. Farben Industrie chemical and substitute war material plants at Ludwigshafen and the engineering and transport industries in the twin city of Mannheim. Stewart led 48 B-24s of the 445th to Ludwigshafen. As the bomb doors opened, a shell burst directly under his wing, but Stewart managed to

A 445th Bomb Group B-24 and some ubiquitous bicycles at Tibenham in 1944. (USAF)

Lieutenant James M. Dodson's B-24H 42-95308 of the 702nd
Bomb Squadron, 445th Bomb Group, landed back at Tibenham
using parachutes as brakes after its hydraulic system had been
shot out over Germany. Fastened to the waist gun positions, the
parachutes were deployed through the windows just before
the wheels touched. This aircraft was written off after a crash on
15 September 1944. (USAF)

regain control and complete the bomb run. After the target he
joined the wayward 389th Bomb Group, which had strayed off
course and although eight 389th B-24s were lost, his action probably prevented that group from total annihilation. On 20 January
1944 he was promoted to major and he took command of the
703rd Bomb Squadron. Next day he led the 445th Bomb Group
to Bonnier, France and the 2nd CBW to Frankfurt on the 29th.
During the 'Big Week' series of missions in February 1944 he led
twenty-eight Liberators of the 445th in the leading 2nd CBW to
Brunswick on Sunday, 20 February. On this raid visual bombing
was impossible so Stewart assumed the lead position an in spite
of aggressive fighter attacks and later heavy anti-aircraft fire,
held the formation together and directed an accurate bombing
run over the target. The 445th lost three Liberators to flak.
Stewart's actions earned him the DFC. On 22 March he led the
wing again, this time to Berlin. This was his first trip to 'Big-B'
and, when asked by newsmen if it was any more unusual than
his others, Stewart said, "Unusual? We hit Berlin, didn't we?' By
now the 'top brass' considered that Stewart had been flying too
many missions and he was moved on 30 March to the 453rd
Bomb Group at Old Buckenham, Norfolk, as Operations Officer.

B-24 Liberators of the 445th Bomb Group *en route* to enemy installations at Glinde, Germany, on 6 October 1944. (USAF)

The 445th Bomb Group flew 282 missions from the airfield with the loss of 133 bombers, including 108 in action. This included the loss, in the space of just six minutes, of twenty-five bombers in action on 27 September 1944 during the raid on the Henschel engine and vehicle assembly plants at Kassel in central Germany. (Five more of the group B-24s crashed in France and England and only five made it back to Tibenham.) This was the highest loss of any 8th AF group in the war.

The 445th received a Distinguished Unit Citation for the 30 September mission and also the Croix de Guerre for assisting French Resistance operations. In the three months after D-Day, 6 June 1944, the group demonstrated the greatest bombing accuracy of any B-24 group in the 8th AF and an above average bombing accuracy for the last six months of the war.

The 445th Bomb Group left Tibenham in May and June 1945 and on 15 July the airfield reverted to the Air Ministry, becoming

an MU satellite. Part was sold off in 1952 but in 1955 the main
runway was lengthened northwards for possible emergency use
by jet aircraft. No units were assigned to the station, however,
and it was eventually closed on 15 March 1959. In 1964–5 the
airfield was sold, and H. Minns demolished most of the buildings, including the hangars. The Norfolk Gliding Club began
using the field in 1960 and now uses the main runway and part
of the east-west one. The control tower was used as a clubhouse
until 1975. Later that year the Norfolk Gliding Club moved into
a new home which was built nearby. It was said that the old
control tower was haunted and several members of the club
were afraid to enter the building, even in daylight! It was said
that a man in flying clothes like those worn by American bomber
crew had been seen on several occasions wandering through the
darkened rooms. In any event, in January 1978 the control tower
was demolished.

WENDLING (STATION 118)

Originally, the airfield at Wendling, in the parish of Beeston near
East Dereham, was intended for RAF bomber use but in 1943 it
was turned over to the 8th AF. It was built by Taylor-Woodrow
Ltd in 1942 and comprised a main north-east–south-west
runway, 2,000 yards long, and two intersecting runways, both
1,400 yards long, with a perimeter track and twenty loop type
and thirty frying-pan type hardstands. Two T2-type hangars
were erected and dispersed accommodation provided for 2,900
men. The domestic sites were in the parish of Beeston to the west
of the airfield and the bomb dump and ammunition stores were
in Honeypot Wood to the south-east. The airfield awaited the
arrival, in the summer of 1943 of the Liberators of the 392nd
Bomb Group, which had been activated at Davis-Monthan Field,
Arizona, on 26 January 1943. On 18 July the ground echelon
sailed from New York for Scotland. On 15 August the air
echelon, led by the CO of the group, Colonel Irvine A. Rendle,
landed at Station 118 with its B-24H and J Liberators, which
differed principally from earlier models in England in having a
power-operated nose turret. The group flew its first combat
mission on 6 September 1943 when the Liberators made a diversionary sweep to aid Fortresses attacking Stuttgart. The first full

Wendling airfield today. (Author)

Their tour over, 392nd personnel wave goodbye to their
buddies at Wendling. (Myran Keilman)

Wendling airfield in March 1946, showing the living sites to the left and the bomb dump stretching away into Honeypot Wood on the right. Top left is the village of Beeston. (USAF)

mission occurred three days later with a raid on Abbeville, France.

Colonel Robert H. Tays was a pilot in the 392nd Bomb Group and recalls life at Wendling.

> Once a month, we had a party at the officers' club. Eight or ten trucks were sent to the neighboring villages to pick up the young ladies that were eager to entertain or be entertained by those daring combatants. Americans seemed to fascinate these gals. Many of them would love to have married an American and come stateside or as they would put it, move to the colonies. A good meal was served, followed by dancing and a floorshow. One show that I remember particularly was a take-off on Carmen Miranda. This person wore the loud gaudy and revealing dress to a tee. Head decorations included the entire fruit world. Her dances were perfect imitations, exotic, provocative, and exuberant. After her performance, a major on the Wing General Staff made a hard play for her. We watched this

B-24H 42-7466 *Ford's Folly* of the 578th Bomb Squadron, 392nd
Bomb Group, is loaded up with incendiary bombs for the
Liberator's 100th mission, on D-Day, 6 June 1944. (USAF)

with the knowledge that the lady was not a lady but a very
young MP from another outfit. When the major had
pressed luck as far as the MP could stand it, he was told the
truth about the disguise – what a surprise with much
embarrassment. Parties needed hoaxes like this. It rounded
out the life style of combat fliers of airplanes, alcohol and
sex. USO shows came to us in the hanger, about once a
month. Bob Hope, Glenn Miller and many more, a host of
comely young gals with each entertainer. The shows were
clean and much fun with GI participation. For an hour or
two, we forgot that we were scheduled to fly tomorrow. A
touch of home or something familiar always seemed to
lighten the stress load. Glenn Miller played our base just a
few days before he was lost. Special parties that lasted all
day were the 100th mission and 200th mission party. We
were stood down by Wing on those special days. Visited by
upper echelon brass from Eighth Air Force and British
civilian dignitaries. The day was filled with parades,
athletic events, good food, drink, dance, and endless flying

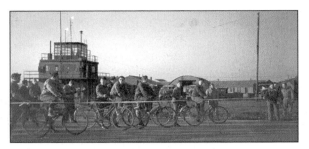

Cycle race at Wendling. (via Ben Jones)

stories. Just another way to make us feel proud of our accomplishments and motivate us to continue to do better. Recognition and the personal touch by the higher up developed a form of camaraderie that exists to this day.

During 'Big Week' on 22 February 1944, the 392nd led the 14th Wing when the 2nd Bomb Division went to bomb the Messerschmitt Bf 110 plant at Gotha. Strung out and in trail, and with some B-24s slowed down because of flak damage, the 392nd was subjected to vicious fighter attacks. For an hour after bombing the group was subjected to head-on passes and tail attacks from singles and gaggles of *Luftwaffe* fighters, and seven

B-24 42-7466 *Ford's Folly* in the 578th BS at Wendling. (USAF)

B-24 *Pallas Athene* being christened at Wendling. (USAF)

392nd personnel at Wendling. (via Ben Jones)

B-24H 42-7466/N *Ford's Folly*, a 578th Bomb Squadron, 392nd
Bomb Group, Liberator being refuelled at Wendling on 9
September 1943 for the group's first combat mission. The group
was equipped with new B-24H and B-24J Liberators fitted with
power-operated nose-gun turrets. Three days earlier, on 6
September, sixty-nine Liberators, including the 392nd, flew a
diversionary sweep over the North Sea for the Fortresses
attacking Stuttgart. (USAF)

Liberators were lost. Another thirteen landed with varying
degrees of damage. The 392nd were extremely accurate, dropping 98 per cent of its bombs within 2,000 feet of the aiming
point, the average percentage of bombs dropped by the 2nd
Bomb Division which fell within 2,000 feet on usual missions
under good to fair visibility in February 1944 was only 49 per
cent. American intelligence described Gotha as the 'most valuable single target in the enemy twin-engine fighter complex.'
The 392nd Bomb Group was awarded a Distinguished Unit
Citation for its part in the raid.

On 4 March 1944 six B-24s of the 392nd Bomb Group bombed
Zurich in Switzerland by mistake during a mission to a
secondary target at Frieburg about 44 miles away. (The 466th
Bomb Group also bombed Basle in error). The 392nd was stood
down for two days, resuming missions on 7 March. The US
Ambassador had only recently attended a memorial service and
visited reconstruction projects of the previous bombing on 18

September 1944. General Marshall urged General Spaatz to visit Switzerland secretly and reparations involving many millions of dollars were made to the Swiss government. In all the 392nd flew a total of 285 operations, losing 184 B-24s and 1,553 crewmen killed. The last mission was flown on 25 April 1945, when the group went to Hallein, Austria. On 25 June Wendling was transferred to RAF Maintenance Command and it was used as a satellite airfield before becoming inactive and closing on 22 November 1961. The airfield was sold between 1963 and 1964, and became a Bernard Matthews turkey farm, with long turkey sheds being constructed on the runways.

APPENDIX 1

Summary of Airfields and Locations

THE 2ND AIR DIVISION USAAF MEMORIAL LIBRARY

The Forum, Millennium Plain, Norwich, Norfolk, NR2 lAW.
Reception desk and enquiries: Tel: 01603 774747.
Trust librarian's office: Tel: 01603 774748. Fax: 01603 774749.
e.mail address: 2admemorial.lib@norfolk.gov.uk
web site: www.2ndair.org.uk
Description: The outstanding new Millennium Building, known as the Forum, includes the Central Library, the 2nd Air Division USAAF Memorial Library, the Heritage Visitor Attraction Centre, Tourist Information and Visitor Centre, Learning Shop and Centre, restaurant, coffee shop and bar, BBC Radio and television studios and an underground car park (entrance from Bethel Street).
Location: The complex adjoins Norwich City Hall and the Church of St Peter Mancroft in the city centre. It lies between Bethel Street and Theatre Street.
Comments: Over 6,700 young Americans of the 2nd AD died flying from English airfields in the Second World War. When the war in Europe drew to a close in early 1945, three senior officers of the division, one from Division HQ, one from the 2nd CBW

The imposing Norwich Forum building, which houses the 2nd
AD Memorial Library viewed from the top of the City Hall.
(Author)

and one from the 467th Bomb Group conceived the idea of establishing a memorial not only to those airmen who flying from bases in these parts gave their lives defending freedom, but also to the survivors. It would also recognise the special bonds of friendship which they had formed with the people of East Anglia.

An appeal was launched to which all ranks of the division could subscribe. It had the enthusiastic support of the Commanding General, William E. Kepner, and in less than a month raised the then amazing sum of £21,000. The newly formed Memorial Trust held its inaugural meeting on 3 July 1945 with American and Norfolk governors. The intention was to utilize the funds to build an archway to the new Central Public Library that Norwich hoped to construct after the war.

Post-war shortages and building priorities resulted in the library not being opened until 1963. The governors of the Memorial Trust had agreed, in consultation with the 2nd Air Division Association in the United States, that the Memorial should take the form of a living Memorial Library. This would be situated in the new Public Library and display the 2nd AD's Roll of Honour and Book of Remembrance and standards. The library itself would have an extensive range of books covering all aspects of American life and history and house the 2nd AD archives. Its aim was to be a haven of peace for future generations to enjoy. This memorial, the only one in the world, was opened by the Minister at the United States Embassy in London, representing the Ambassador, who had been urgently recalled for consultations to Washington and was unable to be present at this memorable occasion on 13 June 1963.

The library rapidly became a treasured part of Norfolk life, and was also the focal point for all occasions when the 2nd Air Division Association returned to Norwich for their conventions. Video and oral history collections were later added to the book collection and in early 1994 the library was enlarged and improved.

Disaster struck on the 1 August 1994 when the entire Norwich Central Library was ravaged by fire. The Memorial Library was totally destroyed, along with all its contents save for the majority of its archives, which thankfully survived. It moved to a temporary public library created in a former furniture showroom in Ber Street, Norwich, pending the construction of a magnificent new £60 million Norfolk and Norwich Millennium Library on the site of the old one. This complex has been supported by a £30 million grant from the Millennium Commission with matching funds from the Norfolk County Council, Norwich City Council and other local sources. Sir Michael Hopkin's renowned firm of architects has designed the new building.

The new Memorial Library is twice as large as the former one, 2,000 square feet in area. It has a book collection of more than 4,000 volumes, covering a wide range of subjects, as in the former library. The Shrine Area, as befits this is an official war memorial, is designed to be a place for calm, peaceful reflection and meditation. Here is the Roll of Honour, listing all those who lost their lives in the line of duty between 1942 and 1945. The large photograph of the American Cemetery at Madingley, where so many members of the 2nd AD, who lost their lives were laid to rest, shows rows of crosses and stars of David reflecting the Christian and Jewish backgrounds of those who made the supreme sacrifice. The three standards and the banners of each bomb group bring colour and warmth to this otherwise tranquil area. Its principal feature is a mural, over 28 feet long, depicting aspects of the 'Friendly Invasion'. Examples of each of the group's aircraft are illustrated in the profile drawings so meticulously executed and given by Mike Bailey. The magnificent large-scale model B-24 Liberator suspended from the ceiling has been generously donated by 2nd AD Veteran Mike Caputo of Meachville, Pennsylvania. Geoffrey Wright spent thousands of hours making models of each group's assembly ships. These aircraft were multicoloured and devised to facilitate formation assembly from each group when light on murky mornings was poor or when there was bright, low sun. In these conditions it was difficult for pilots to distinguish the markings on the wings and vertical tail fins of aircraft belonging to their group. Mr Wright has kindly made all these magnificent models available to the Memorial Trust on permanent loan.

The trust librarians and the library enquiry assistants can direct visitors to the individual records of each group and deal with any general enquiries. The Memorial Library has its own extensive web site and there are computer links to other parts of the adjoining main library, which has one of the most innovative IT systems of any library in Europe. The Memorial Library has its own B-24 flight simulator, the first of its kind in the world, on which visitors are able to participate in virtual-reality flights.

City of Norwich Aviation Museum (CONAM)

Old Norwich Road, Horsham St Faith, Norwich NR10 3JF.
Tel 01603 893080
Description: Aviation museum featuring the 100 Group Memorial Room and historical aircraft and exhibits.
Location: On the northern edge of Norwich International Airport (formerly RAF Horsham St Faith), which offers a good view of the passenger aircraft flying from this expanding regional airport.
Directions: Leaving Norwich take the A140 towards Cromer and turn right off the bypass after the main airport entrance.
Comments: No trip to the region's airfields and tourist attractions is complete without rounding everything off or starting with a visit to this museum, which was conceived and is run by

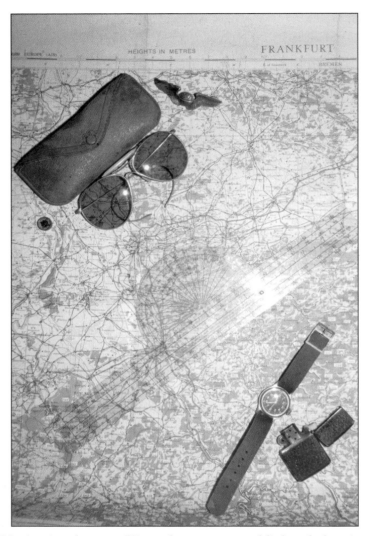

Navigational maps, GI watch, compass and lighter belonging to Lieutenant Robert A. Jacobs of the 389th Bomb Group on display at the City of Norwich Aviation Museum near Norwich Airport. Jacobs was a DR navigator on *Liberty Run*, the 389th Bomb Group PFF ship, which was the first B-24 over the beaches on D-Day, 6 June 1944. (Author)

a dedicated band of volunteers. A Vulcan bomber dominates it's collection and a variety of other aircraft, both civilian and military, are also on display. Within the exhibition building are displays showing the development of aviation in Norfolk. There are special displays relating to the 458th Bomb Group and other units which served at the airfield during the war and after. Pride of place has to go to the Stafford Sinclair Room, which is dedicated to the operations of 100 Group RAF. An excellent gift shop sells books, models and other items. Opening Times: April–October, Tuesday–Saturday 10.00–5.00, Sundays and bank holidays 1200–5.00, school holidays, 1200–5.00; November–March: Wednesday and Saturday 10.00–4.00, Sundays and bank holidays 12.00–4.00. Closed over Christmas and New Year. Admission prices vary. Children under 5 free.

Attlebridge (Station 120)

Description: American bomber base used by the 466th Bomb Group in the Second World War.
Location: about 8 miles north-west of Norwich.
Directions: Follow the A47 Norwich–Dereham road to Weston Longville.

Huts at Attlebridge in 1953. (Mort Meinteinsma)

Comments: For many years the Liberator Bar in the Five Ringers at Weston Longville housed many 466th Bomb Group artifacts. The pub was sold and closed in 1987 for refurbishment and it reopened as the Parson Woodforde, named after the rector of the parish 1775–1803. Much of the memorabilia displayed in the pub was put on the walls of an office in the control tower at the old base, which has been used as offices since 1958 by Bernard

Huts at Attlebridge in 1953. (Mort Meinteinsma)

Attlebridge control tower in 1953. (Mort Meinteinsma)

Matthews Ltd, by Mrs Jenny Staff, who worked for Matthews until September 1988. When she left she moved the items to her home at 3 The Green, Weston Longville, on the edge of a hard-standing (it still has tie-down rings for aircraft). Later, the memorabilia, including photos, a Stars and Stripes flag, plaques and models of B-24s, was moved to Pond Farm's domestic accommodation, the former headquarters building which the

The windmill near Weston Longville. B-24 crews would buzz it and spin its sails in 1944–45. (Author)

Aerial view of Attlebridge airfield showing the turkey sheds on the runways. (Author)

Thomson family bought in 1980 and converted into a home. The briefing room and the office annexe, both big Nissen huts near the rear of the station HQ building, had many uses after the war. In 1989 they were cleaned up and used for general storage. The brick bombsight store was converted into a bungalow early in 1990. A quarter of a mile from the administration site, the floors of the hospital remain. There are remnants of the theatre and the mess hall, too. Some motor pool buildings survive and are used by a farmer. Outlying buildings still standing are overgrown. The T2 hangars have long since been taken down.

In All Saints Church, Weston Longville, is a Roll of Honour for the 466th, covering the period 22 January 1944 to 21 April 1945. It is also remembered on the Weston Longville village ornamental sign positioned at the roadside outside the church. It was donated and erected by the 466th Bomb Group Association in 1977 and dedicated on 9 June 1984. It has the outline shape of a B-24 fin and rudder. A plaque on the pole says: 'Presented to the people of Weston Longville 27 August 1977 by the 466th Bomb Group US 8th AF in memory of the 324 men from this group killed in action flying from the airfield in this parish

A wartime hut and a turkey shed behind at Attlebridge in the winter of 2002. (Author)

Aerial view of Attlebridge airfield showing the turkey sheds on the runways. (Author)

Memorial to the 466th Bomb Group at Attlebridge airfield. (Author)

March 1944–May 1945.' On 12 June 1992 a marble stone memorial to the memory of the 466th Bomb Group was unveiled on the southern side of the airfield near Franz Green. Built into the wall at the rear of the memorial are the four squadron badges.

Unit	From	To	Aircraft	Squadron Codes
466th Bomb Group 784th, 785th, 786th, 787th Bomb Squadrons	7 March 1944	6 July 1945	B-24H/J/L/M Liberator	T9 ZU U8 6L

BUNGAY (FLIXTON) (STATION 125)

Description: American bomber base used by the 446th Bomb Group in the Second World War.
Location: On a plateau above the Waveney Valley about 2 miles south-west of Bungay and just beyond the village of Flixton.
Directions: Take the B1062 from Bungay and head south towards the Norfolk and Suffolk Aviation Museum at Flixton.
Comments: Before the 446th left the airfield in July 1945 it presented a set of wooden gates to St Mary's Church, Flixton,

American Air Force memorabilia on display at the Norfolk and Suffolk Aviation Museum at Flixton. (Author)

The Norfolk and Suffolk Aviation Museum at Flixton viewed
through the nose of the BBMF Lancaster. (Author)

Map of the USA on a wall at Flixton. The Yanks, as they were universally known, came from the big cities and the back-woods, up state and downtown, from California to Connecticut, Delaware to Dakota, Frisco to Florida, Mid-West to Maine, New York, New England, Ohio and Hawaii, the Pacific, and way beyond. (Author)

706th Squadron badge and mural at Flixton. (Author)

704th Bomb
Squadron badge
on a wall at
Bungay (Flixton)
in 1991. (Author)

which stands close to the old airfield. In the spring of 1986 a new set of oak gates raised by donations from veterans of the 446th Bomb Group were hung at St Mary's Church and in 1987 during a 2nd Air Division Association reunion the gates were dedicated and a Roll of Honour placed in the church. A small memorial plaque carries the inscription: 'These gates were presented in memory of the men of the 446th Bombardment Group, USAAF, who gave their lives in defence of freedom, 1941–1945'. Little of the airfield remains, although some buildings such as the staff canteen at the Buxted chicken factory still stand. On one of its walls is a memorial plaque to the 446th Bombardment Group. The inscription on the plaque says: 'This plaque was unveiled by Major-General Evan W. Rosencrans on Monday 20th May 1974 to commemorate those American airmen who flew out of Flixton (The Bungay Buckaroos) 1943–45'.

Another plaque dedicated to the 446th is in the Community Centre in Upper Olland Street, Bungay. This was dedicated in May 1983. A notice board made of oak was placed in the Church of England primary school at Flixton in 1978 as a memorial to Sergeant Jimmy Seery, who established a strong rapport with the local children. The bond ended only when he had a heart attack and died in a Chicago hospital when travelling to England for a reunion in the 1970s. At the end of the 1988 summer term the school closed down permanently. The notice board was moved to the church for safekeeping until it could go in the village hall after roof repairs.

About eight Nissen huts on the Buxted site are used for storage. Part of the officers' mess was on the site. Brick buildings on the adjoining farm site were also part of the base. There are several fine examples of wall art, which include 446th Bomb Group inspired works and some from the immediate post-war period including a beautiful mermaid and sailor painting. This must emanate from the winter of 1945–46 when Flixton became HMS *Europa*, a satellite of HMS *Sparrowhawk* (Halesworth) where three FAA squadrons were based. *See also: Norfolk & Suffolk Aviation Museum Flixton.*

Unit	From	To	Aircraft	Squadron Codes
446th Bomb Group 704th, 705th, 706th, 707th Bomb Squadrons	4 November 1943	5 July 1945	B-24H/L/M	FL HN RT JU

HALESWORTH (STATION 365)

Description: American base used by the 56th Fighter Group and the 489th Bomb Group in the Second World War.
Location: In the village of Holton, between the A144 and B1124 roads about 2 miles north-east of the market town of Halesworth.
Directions: Follow A144 from Halesworth to the roundabout with A144 Bungay road and Triple Plea public house, and follow the road around to the airfield. Alternatively, follow the B1124 Beccles road and turn left to Holton airfield. The 489th Bomb Group memorial is in front of the Bernard Matthews factory and the museum is on the same road.

The 489th Bomb Group memorial at Halesworth (Holton) airfield. (Author)

Comments: The superb Holton Airfield Museum is housed in an original Second World War building on the old communal site donated by Bernard Matthews Ltd. The Halesworth Memorial Asssociation was formed late in 1996 with the ambition of opening a museum dedicated to the 56th Fighter Group, which served at the airfield from July 1943 to April 1944. The museum opened in August 1997. Although most of the contents cover the 56th Fighter Group there are many added exhibits of interest related to the Second World War. Opening times are Sundays and bank holidays, 2.00–5.00 pm, admission free. Nearby is a polished marble stone with a plan view of the runways and perimeter track and an 8th AF badge was erected on the old airfield. The inscription reads: 'Dedicated to all who served here with the 489th Bomb Group (USAAF) especially to those who gave their lives in the cause of freedom and human dignity.'

Further along the road on a grassy bank in front of former wartime buildings is a fighter drop tank. Painted on it are the words: 'USAAF Station 305, Halesworth, 95th Air Wing, 8th Air Force. 56th Fighter Group July 1943 to April 1944. 489th Bomb Group May 1944 to Nov 1944. 5th ERS Jan 1945 to May 1945. 496th FTG March to May 1945.' Three aircraft are also painted on the tank, representing units based here.

On a memorial stone in Ashby St Mary churchyard off an unclassified road 1 mile north of Somerleyton are the names of Lieutenant Russel P. Judd and Flight Officer Louis S. Davis of the 5th ERS (and four names of a 100th Bomb Group B-17 crew). Judd and Davis died when their P-47Ds collided over Fritton Lake on 8 April 1945 during mock combat after an ASR patrol.

Unit	From	To	Aircraft	Squadron Codes
489th Bomb Group, 844th, 845th, 846th 847th Bomb Squadrons	1 May 1944	28 November 1944	B-24H/J Liberator	4R T4 8R S4

HARDWICK (STATION 104)

Description: American bomber base used by the 93rd Bomb Group in the Second World War.
Location: 5 miles west of the A140 Norwich–Ipswich road, and 11 miles south of Norwich.
Directions: From Norwich take the A140 and at Tasburgh (8 miles) turn left taking the B1135 signed Bungay. After 2½ miles pass through Hempnall and after ½ mile turn right into Alburgh Road. After 1½ miles, after passing through Hempnall Green, the road leads onto the northern edge of the airfield before bending to follow its eastern edge. From the south, using the A140, pass through Long Stratton and after 1½ miles turn right onto the B1135 Bungay road and proceed as above. From the Bungay direction (east and south-east), take the B1332 Norwich–Bungay road turning left at Woodton 3½ miles onto the B1335 and after 3 miles turn left into Alburgh Road as above.
Comments: Parts of the runways and perimeter track and some buildings remain. A P-51D Mustang owned by Maurice Hammond is based at the airfield and is flown on a regular basis. Four brick and cement Nissen huts, which formed part of the communal site for the 329th Bomb Squadron, remain in the area

Hardwick airfield viewed though the nose of the BBMF
Lancaster in September 1999. (Author)

Bob Shaffer, who
flew missions in
the 93rd Bomb
Group, reminisces
by the old fire
pool at Hardwick
in the 1970s.
(Author)

east of the airfield, but these are not visible from the public highways. These buildings have been restored and three form a small museum. Hut 1 houses USAAF uniforms and photographs, together with artifacts recovered from crash sites. Hut 2 is dedicated to the RAF. Uniforms are displayed together with items such as a Lancaster wing tip and part of a Stirling tail. Hut 3 is dedicated to the 409th Bomb Squadron. A black granite memorial erected by veterans of the 93rd Group stands on a piece of land which was once part of the wartime Hardwick airfield. The inscription reads:

93rd Bombardment Group (Heavy) 328th, 329th, 330th and 409th Bombardment Squadrons and attached units, 20th Combat Wing Second Air Division 8th United States Army Air Force. From this airfield and others in England and North Africa, the 93rd Group flew a total of 391 combat missions in support of the Allied war effort during World War II. These missions were flown from 9 October 1942 until 25 April 1945. This monument is dedicated to the memory of those lost in the war and to the survivors who helped achieve ultimate peace and victory. Two Medals of Honor. Two Presidential Unit Citations: North Africa and Ploesti. Battles and Campaigns: American Theater. Antisubmarine ATO. Air Combat-EAME Theater. Air Offensive-Europe. Anti-submarine-ETO. Egypt-Libya. Ploesti. Tunisia. Naples-Foggia. Sicily. Normandy. Northern France. Rhineland. Ardennes-Alsace. Central Europe. Dedicated 25 May 1987.

Group and squadron badges appear on the memorial as well as views of the B-24 Liberator.

The buildings, museum and memorial can normally be viewed on the third Sunday of each month, May–October 10.00–5.00 or by appointment with the landowner, Mr David Woodrow (Tel: 01508 482263), admission free, refreshments available.

Unit	From	To	Aircraft	Squadron Codes
93rd Bomb Group 328th, 329th, 330th, 409th Bomb Squadrons	6 December 1942	12 June 1945	B-24D/E/H/J/L/M Liberator	GO RE AG YM

Hethel (Station 114)

Description: American bomber base used by the 389th Bomb Group in the Second World War.

Location: 7 miles south-west of Norwich and 3 miles east of Wymondham, which lies on the A11 Norwich–Newmarket road.

Directions: To reach Hethel from Norwich, use the A11 or the B1135 Norwich–New Buckenham road. Taking the A11 from Norwich, turn right at Wymondham at the traffic-lighted junction with the B1135. Proceed straight across the Fairlands

Hethel airfield in the 1970s. (Author)

Passing the control tower and Lotus factory in June 1993. (Author)

and then turn right after the police station into Browick Road. Cross the railway and after 1 mile bear right past the oil storage depot, which after 2½ miles skirts the southern boundary of the airfield. Continue and turn left on to Potash Lane (signed 'Lotus Cars') which skirts the eastern boundary of the airfield and gives access to the Lotus Car Company. (The road northwards to a T-junction and left into St Thomas Lane, which skirts the northern edge of the field, has been closed by Lotus.) Using the B1113, pass through the villages of Mulbarton and Bracon Ash and 2½ miles past Bracon Ash turn right into the minor road signed Hethel and after ½ mile the southern boundary of the airfield and Potash Lane are reached. From a southerly direction, using the A11, at Wymondham, turn left at the traffic-lighted junction with the B1135, cross the Fairlands and follow the directions above.

Comments: In 1944 wood from the choir stall in front of the

Leper's Window in the Lady Chapel in All Saints Church at Carleton Rode was used for a memorial plaque, which was unveiled in June 1946 to commemorate seventeen members of the 389th killed on 21 November 1944 when B-24J 42-50452 *Earthquake McGoon* of the 566th Bomb Squadron flown by Lieutenant Alfred Brooks and B-24J 44-10513 of the 565th Bomb Squadron, flown by First Lieutenant James Rhine, collided shortly after take-off from Hethel for the mission to Hamburg. Both aircraft came down in the parish of Carleton. Brooks was the only survivor from *Earthquake McGoon*. Two of Rhine's crew, Lieutenant W Martin, the bombardier, and Sergeant P. Ferdinand, the radio operator, survived the crash. Since 1946 a wreath has been laid in the church by a USAF officer from RAF Lakenheath at the Service of Remembrance held in November each year.

The completely restored chapel at Hethel showing the crucifixion scene on the wall behind the altar, which Charles 'Bud' Doyle painted in February/March 1944. During restoration, the restorers found another religious figure under a coat of white paint (right). (Author)

389th Bomb Group 'Sky Scorpion' veterans in 1983 outside the Green Dragon pub in Wymondham, Norfolk, which was used as the name for the Group's assembly ship and the unit insignia. Far left is Earl Zimmerman, Jack Cox, Far right is Russ D. Hayes who was a gunner on *The Little Gramper*. (Author)

Lotus Car Company constructed a factory on the former technical site, which lies on the eastern side of the airfield. The three hangars have been extensively refurbished (one has been slightly moved) and now form part of the factory. The associated car test track uses parts of the north-east–south-west and the north-west–south-east runways. At the northern end of the airfield there is a black T2 hangar adjacent to St Thomas Lane. This hangar, which came from another airfield, was re-erected on this site in the mid-1960s. (it is no longer possible to gain access from Potash Lane to St Thomas Lane, which has been sealed off.) The three T2 hangars on the former technical site remain but have been extensively refurbished. Behind woodland off Potash Lane opposite the technical site, a dedicated team of volunteers have worked tirelessly to renovate the chapel building to its former status. Once the chapel was the domain of

Father Gerald Beck, the Catholic group chaplain at Hethel. Now visitors can view the chapel and its colourful wartime map of Europe and the crucifixion scene. During restoration there was an unexpected bonus when paint was removed to reveal the image of the Madonna. For further information on the renovated chapel, please contact Fred Squires, 34 Park Close, Silfield, Wymondham, Norfolk NR18 9BA. Telephone 01953 607147.

In the United Reformed church at Wymondham is a plaque, bought by the air gunners of the 389th Bomb Group, in memory of the Protestant chaplain at Hethel, Captain Earl O. Widen. He also ministered at the local church after the sudden death of the parishioners' own minister. The combination of military duties and his voluntary commitments proved too much and he died late in 1944. The Wymondham congregation sent a plaque in his memory to his home church, the Bethlehem Baptist Church in Minneapolis. *See also Ketteringham Hall and Wymondham.*

Unit	From	To	Aircraft	Squadron Codes
389th Bomb Group 564th, 565th, 566th, 567th Bomb Squadrons	11 June 1943	30 May 1945	B-24D/E/H/J/L/M Liberator	YO EE RR HP

HORSHAM ST FAITH (STATION 123)

Description: RAF airfield transferred to the 8th Air Force for use by P-47 Thunderbolt fighters of the 56th Fighter Group and B-24 Liberator bombers of the 458th Bomb Group in the Second World War. Now Norwich International Airport.

Location: On the A140 northbound Norwich–Cromer road.

Directions: Follow the road signs to Norwich Airport from the city centre and ring road.

Comments: Many of the wartime buildings and three of the original hangars remain because the airfield is now Norwich Airport and also an industrial complex. The former barracks and officers mess buildings off Fifers Lane, which were used for a time as accommodation for students attending the University of East Anglia, have now been demolished to make way for housing. The former RAF married quarters and the officer housing in Fifers Lane are now private residences. A memorial stone to the 458th Bomb Group has been erected next to the main passenger terminal at the airport. In Church Street, Old Catton,

The 'Cat on the Barrel' village sign in Church Street, Old Catton, Norwich. (Author)

near the airport is the famous wood carved Cat on the Barrel village sign. The cat perched atop the post is reported to have been flown aloft in B-24 Liberators of the 458th Bomb Group in the Second World War. In Church Street is a tablet in the wall commemorating the 'loss of twenty valuable lives' of B-24H 42-94811 *Tommy Thumper II* of the 790th Bomb Squadron, 467th Bomb Group, which crashed just off Church Street during a training flight from Rackheath on 22 January 1945, and B-24J

The former Horsham St Faith officer's mess off Fifers Lane, Hellesdon, which has been demolished to make way for a housing development. (Author)

On 22 January 1945 B-24H 42-94811 *Tommy Thumper II* of the 790th Bomb Squadron, 467th Bomb Group, piloted by Flight Officer John McArthur, crashed on a training flight from Rackheath, at Old Catton,  Norwich, while attempting to land at Horsham St Faith. Having lost one engine McArthur had then accidentally feathered the other engine on the same wing, causing the B-24 to spin in and crash in a large estate just off Church Street. (James J. Mahoney)

44-40281 *A Dog's Life*, which crashed at the junction of Spixworth Road and Church Street on 13 February 1945.

In the airport terminal is a memorial display to the 458th Bomb Group which includes photographs, the badges of the four squadrons assigned to the group and a bronze plaque inscribed: 'Dedicated in memory of the 458th Bombardment Group (H) USAAF Horsham St. Faith January 1944–June 1945.' Fixed to the wall of flats in Watson Grove, facing Heigham Street, there is a plaque to the memory of Second Lieutenant Ralph J. Dooley's crew of the 753rd Squadron, who died when they crashed in the old corporation yard in Barker Street, just off Heigham Street, on 24 November 1944. The tablet was originally mounted on the wall of a house on the north side of Heigham Street but was resited upon redevelopment in 1972. A memorial

The Heigham Street plaque in memory of the Dooley crew in Norwich. (Author)

The ill-fated Dooley crew. Second-Lieutenant Dooley far right.
(USAF)

tablet also commemorates the crew of B-24 44-40283 *Lassie Come Home*, which crashed in the back garden of 14 Spynke Road near 'The Boundary', on 11 January 1945. *See also City of Norwich Aviation Museum (CONAM) and the 2nd Air Division USAAF Memorial Library, Norwich.*

Unit	From	To	Aircraft	Squadron Codes
458th Bomb Group 752nd, 753rd, 754th 755th Bomb Squadrons	29 January 1944	3 July 1945	B-24J/L/M Liberator	7V J4 Z5 J3

Ketteringham Hall (Station 147)

Description: 2nd Bomb/Air Division Headquarters December 1943–June 1945.
Location: 7½ miles to the south-west of Norwich near to Hethel airfield.
Directions: Follow the A11 and then turn left to Ketteringham village church.

Aerial view of Ketteringham Hall in 1993, the wartime HQ for
the 2nd AD. (Author)

Comments: Ketteringham Hall has been described as a 'noble
mansion' and is said to have been built on a Tudor core, a period
in English history dating from 1485 to 1603. It stands on
Ketteringham Park estate, which dates back to the time of
Edward the Confessor, the Anglo-Saxon King of 1004–66. The
estate appears in the Doomsday Book, a survey of England
completed in 1088 on the instruction of King William I (1066–87),
who instigated an 'efficient government and controlled the
barons'. The Hall is reputed to have been the childhood home of
England's shortest reigning monarch, Lady Jane Grey
(1537–1554), daughter of the Duke of Suffolk and great grand-
daughter of King Henry VII. John Peter Boileau was responsible
for Ketteringham Hall as it now stands. He bought the estate in
1839 and in 1840 work started on the Gothic hall, integral with
the main building. It was used as a chapel and also a banqueting
room. The ceiling was resplendent with the coat of arms of the
Boileau family – pelican above the family shield and the motto
'*De tout mon couer*'.

   When war was declared Sir Raymond and his wife Ethel,
Lady Boileau (a pre-war best selling authoress) continued to live

Group commanders gather in the gardens at Ketteringham Hall in early March 1944. Back row, left to right: Fred Dent (44th Bomb Group), Milton W. Arnold (389th), Jacob Brogger (446th), Jim Isbell (458th), James Thompson (448th, killed 1 April 1944), Leland Fiegel (93rd), Albert J. Shower (467th), Irvine Rendle (392nd), Ramsey D. Potts (453rd). Front row, left to right: Jack Wood (20th CBW), Ted Timberlake (2nd CBW), Brigadier-General James P. Hodges (CO, 2nd BD), Leon Johnson (14th CBW), Jerry Mason (soon to command the 448th upon the death of Colonel Thompson). (USAF)

at the Hall, Ethel becoming local commandant of the First Aid Nursing Yeomanry (FANY) and Commanding Officer of the complete brigade. Ethel died in 1941, Sir Raymond in 1942. Rachel Boileau, who had looked after Sir Raymond, together with their three children, remained at the Hall. Prior to the Americans moving to their new 2nd AD HQ at Ketteringham Hall in December 1943, a government requisition order instructed the family to move out. Rachel firmly resisted such a suggestion and eventually the arrangement was made that the family could move into a smaller area within the house. (Some of the American servicemen received frequent reprimands for short-cutting through the flowerbeds.) The chapel or Justice

Room became the War Room, a half-floor area mezzanine being constructed with a glass viewing area for high-ranking officers to survey the battle map of Europe spread out below, surrounded by servicemen and women keeping the state of battle right up to date. On the ground floor was the Operations Section, War Room and Intelligence Section. James Stewart, the Hollywood film actor, visited the Hall to give debriefings after completion of missions. One of the former intelligence officers remembered him 'because his reports were so precise, full of accurate detail.' On the first floor, over the main entrance, was the office of the Division Adjutant General. Also on that floor were the offices of the Commanding General, the Chief of Staff and the Deputy Chief of Staff. On the second floor those officers had their quarters and a small dining room.

On his return from the war, and after the Americans left in June 1945, Major Etienne Boileau rejoined his wife Rachel and they continued running the estate, which included the surrounding lands, and the former Hethel airbase. Mrs Angela Boileau, who came to stay with her sister-in-law Rachel at the Hall in 1943 with her year old son, recalled:

> The American officers' mess was directly above our dining room and during lunch one day I saw smoke rising from my small son's pram in which he was sleeping outside. Rushing out I found a cigar thrown out from above had caused it! There were profuse apologies, followed by lots of wonderful American goodies sent to atone. They were such a friendly crowd but even so we were not allowed anywhere near the operations (or war room) centre. However they used to entice the youngest daughter and my son into where all the secrets were and then give them sweets, much to Nanny's great disapproval. They were all very nice and some used to come and see us most evenings to have drinks. After the war when the area in and around the Hall was cleared up, there was a great deal of rotting woodwork in the house as a result of the intense heat the Americans worked in, with their shirt sleeves rolled up in the depths of winter!

Nissen hut in the grounds of Ketteringham Hall. James Cagney
played here in 1944. (Author)

The number of servicemen and women living in the Nissen huts
forming a small village to the rear of the Hall beyond the family
orchard numbered between 300 and 400. The concrete roads and
Nissen hut bases still remain to this day but only one large
Nissen hut remains intact and still in use. It was the 'old opry
house' and James Cagney gave two shows in it. It was also the
venue where many Americans saw their first showing of the
famous Bing Crosby film *White Christmas*, which was shown at
all active service stations before its premiere in the States.

Nancy Stanyer was cook to Mrs Rachel Boileau:

> There were American buildings all over the place. A lot of
> men were obviously missing their families – they just loved
> children and would always give them sweets (which of
> course we never saw normally) and if there was a pram
> standing anywhere you would find two or three of them
> talking to the baby in it. One kept dropping his hat in
> puddles and asking us to wash it – it was obviously his way
> of keeping in touch with ordinary people. They would
> always appear when I baked bread in our old oven – you

Ketteringham Hall near Hethel, which, from December 1943 to June 1945, was used as the 2nd BD (later 2nd AD) HQ. The Hall, which dates from Tudor times, is reputed to have been the childhood home of Lady Jane Grey (1537–1554), England's shortest-reigning monarch. After the war it served as a preparatory school, and it was bought by Lotus Cars in 1968. (USAF)

could smell it half a mile away and they would drop in for a slice or two. We didn't have anything to put on the bread but that didn't bother them. Then they would stand and have a chat. A lot of them were guarding the Hall. All our bicycles, theirs and ours, had numbers stamped on them and we carried photographs of ourselves which acted as passports.

Nancy's husband Stan remembers:

When I came home on leave from the army it was usually late when I got into Norwich and by 10 p.m. the buses had stopped. The Americans used to have a bus leaving from the theatre so I would try to catch that. If I missed it I had to walk the 8 miles home. I used to get really browned off when I got to Ketteringham Hall. I was always in uniform with a kit bag over my shoulder but hadn't got a 'passport' like Nancy and they would always stop and question me. They had a gate at the back entrance near our thatched house [Church House] and a wooden sentry box. I used to go down to Hethel to see the Liberators depart and return. You could always tell there were wounded on board by the flares they let off circling the airfield, and then once they had landed the ground crews and medical people would be there immediately. Most times it certainly was not a nice scene.

Something that always worried us was when the German planes would follow them in when they returned, something they often did. As well as that we had the threat of crippled bombers crashing in the surrounding countryside. One crashed quite near the Hall and another behind some cottages in Bracon Ash [the village bordering Hethel]. A bomb fell by the household refuse dump one day and the lady in a little house tucked away in the corner near it ran out, I suppose to go into her shelter, and dropped dead from shock. We never discovered if it was one of our bombs or one from a German plane but there was a lot of confusion with guns banging away and a tremendous amount of noise.

In 1948 the Hall was sold to the Duke of Westminster, Britain's richest landowner. In 1950 certain parts were occupied by a preparatory school. The school gradually took over more of the Hall until eventually the whole of the building was occupied by 1963. This school continued until 1965 when the Hall was sold to Badingham College Ltd.

When it became vacant in 1968 Lotus acquired the lease and it was designated as 'Colin Chapman's think tank', although the Lotus staff dubbed it 'Fawlty Towers' after the highly popular TV comedy series about a chaotic hotel in the English West Country. Almost immediately the Field Service School moved in, followed by Lotus Car's trim (upholstery) department, providing the top-quality leather seats and ancillary trim for the Lotus road cars. This was to stay for six years, only returning to Hethel when Ketteringham Hall and its refurbished stables area were designated the headquarters of the international motor racing Team Lotus in 1977. It was from here in 1978 that the team won its seventh World Championship Constructors' title with American star Mario Andretti, who won the team's sixth World Championship of Drivers.

On 25 May 1987 a memorial plaque on the wall of the sheltered garden seat beyond the conservatory dedicated to those who served in the 2nd AD in the Second World War was dedicated.

Unit	From	To	Aircraft	Squadron Code
2nd Bomb/Air Division HQ	December 1943	June 1945	None	None

METFIELD (STATION 366)

Description: American base used by the 353rd Fighter Group and the 491st Bomb Group in the Second World War.
Location: 6 miles south-east of Metfield village off the B1123. Harleston–Halesworth road.
Directions: Follow the B1123 to Metfield. The airfield is close by the village.
Comments: Very little remains of this desolate airfield.

Unit	From	To	Aircraft	Squadron Code
491st Bomb Group 852nd, 853rd, 854th, 855th Bomb Squadrons	25 April 1944	15 August 1955	B-24H/J/L/M Liberator	3Q T8 6X V2

NORTH PICKENHAM (STATION 143)

Description: American bomber base used by the 492nd and 491st Bomb Groups in the Second World War.
Location: 2½ miles south-east of Swaffham.
Directions: Follow the A47 and turn off for Swaffham on the A1065 road north before truning onto the B1077, which runs along the southern edge of the former airfield.
Comments: Very little of this desolate airfield remains. A memorial stone to the Americans of the 492nd and 491st Bomb Groups who flew from the airfield in the Second World War can be located near the roadside adjacent to a housing complex near the airfield called Brecklands. A few derelict wartime buidlings can be seen on dispersed sites near the village. On the opposite

Aerial view of the former airfield, now dotted with turkey sheds. (Author)

side of the road to the primary school, set in a small flower garden, is a stone inscribed, 'In memory of the men of the USAAF who flew from North Pickenham 1944–1945, 492nd Bomb Group April 1944–August 1945, 491st Bomb Group, August 1944–May 1945.' There is also a commemorative clock at the church. Inside the Blue Lion public house is a plaque inscribed, 'Presented to North Pickenham village July 9th 1992 by the family of William F. Sheely, 492nd Bomb Gp. (H) 859th Sq. in tribute to the intense aerial combat endured by the 492nd Bomb Group, May–August 1944. Other aviation mementoes are also in the pub.

Unit	From	To	Aircraft	Squadron Codes
492nd Bomb Group 856th, 857th, 858th, 859th Bomb Squadrons	14 April 1944	12 August 1944	B-24H/J Liberator	5Z 9H 9AX4
491st, Bomb Group 852nd, 853rd, 854th, 855th Bomb Squadrons	15 August 1944	4 July 1945	B-24H/J/L/M Liberator	3 Q T8 6X V2
220 Squadron RAF	July 1959	July 1963	Thor IRBM	

NORFOLK & SUFFOLK AVIATION MUSEUM, FLIXTON

Buckaroo Way, The Street, Flixton, near Bungay, Suffolk NR35 1NZ tel. 01986 896644

Description: Several hangar museums on site including the Royal Observer Corps Museum and RAF Bomber Command Museum. Over twenty historical aircraft on display.

Location: Behind the Buck Inn public house.

Directions: Turn off the A143 bypass onto the B1062 old Bungay–Harleston road.

Comments: Refreshments, shop, free parking, nature trail. An unusual bronze statue called 'Scramble' with a pilot and his dog on a plinth is in the open area. Very interesting memorabilia is on show and the venue overall is excellent. Opening times: April–October, Sunday–Thursday and bank holidays 10.00–5.00; November–March, Tuesday, Wednesday and Sunday, 10.00–4.00; closed 15 December–15 January, school summer holidays, Sundays, Tuesdays, Wednesdays and Thursdays 10.00–5.00. Admission free.

OLD BUCKENHAM (STATION 144)

Description: American bomber base used by the 453rd Bomb Group in the Second World War.

Location: 2 miles south-east of Attleborough and the A11 Thetford–Norwich road.

Directions: Follow the A11 Norwich–Attleborough road and turn onto the B1077 at Attleborough, following the winding country road to Old Buckenham village, where a left turn at the common is made into Abbey Road.

Comments: The majority of the old base has disappeared to be replaced by an industrial estate but beside the old main runway, which was broken up and used to create a new 800 metre strip, is the Touchdown Aero Centre, which offers flying and an annual air show. Next to the Touchdown Aero Centre off Abbey Road is an upright memorial in the shape of a B-24 Liberator tail fin and rudder with the diagonal marking of the 453rd Bomb Group. The group's badge, a B-24 and the 8th AF insignia also appears. On the front is an outline of the airfield and the inscription reads:

Aerial view of Old Buckenham and the Touchdown Centre
with its new runway. (Author)

Bill Eagelson,
bombardier of,
'Corky' Burgundy
Bomber in the
733rd Bomb
Squadron, by the
453rd Bomb
Group memorial
in 1992. (Author)

United States Army Air Forces Station 144 Old Buckenham. The 453rd Bombardment Group (H), 2nd Combat Wing, 2nd Air Division, Eighth Air Force, served here December 1943–May 1945. From this airfield B-24 Liberators of 732, 733, 734, and 735 Bombardment Squadrons (H) flew 259 missions, dropped 15,804 tons of bombs, lost 58 aircraft missing in action. 366 aircrew lost their lives. To these brave Americans and to all who served here during World War II this memorial is dedicated. 29th July 1990.

Veterans of the 453rd Bomb Group paid for an extension of the village community hall, which had been built in 1979. The Memorial Room contains wartime photographs, maps, badges, a scrapbook compiled by an American veteran, pieces of aircraft, furlough books, railway tickets, bullets and a large bronze plaque listing those in the 453rd who died on missions. There is also a visitors' book. An album contains photographs of the activities on 30 May 1983 when the extension was opened. Some show film star James Stewart, who served as the Group

Russ Harriman and Frank Thomas, who were on the crew of *Never Mrs*, reminisce in the former operations room at Old Buckenham in the 1970s. (Author)

Bill Eagelson, bombardier of, *'Corky' Burgundy Bomber* in the 733rd Bomb Squadron, 453rd Bomb Group, in the operations block at Old Buckenham in 1992. (Author)

Operations Officer from March to June 1944 before being promoted to lieutenant-colonel and moving to 2nd CBW HQ at Hethel as Chief of Staff. Stewart often starred on stage and in June 1975, while he was performing *Harvey* in London he took the opportunity to visit Norfolk and in particular his old haunts at Tibenham and Old Buckenham. During a visit to Norwich in May 1983 for the 2nd AD reunion he attended the 30 May Memorial Day at Cambridge and at Old Buckenham he also planted a tulip tree outside the community hall extension. A plaque on the wall says: 'The tree opposite was planted to commemorate the opening of the 453rd Bomb Group memorial room 30th May, 1983.' (Stewart died at his home in Beverly Hills on 2 July 1997 aged 89.) Walter Matthau (real name Walter

Matasschanskayasky), who became a leading film actor after the war, was a staff sergeant radio mechanic in the 453rd.

Touchdown Aero Centre is at Abbey Road, Old Buckenham, NR17 1PU. Tel. 01953 860806. A/G Frequency 124.40. Local contact for the former Station 144 is Mr Pat Ramm, Common Farm, Little Ellingham, Attleborough, Norfolk, NR17 1JU. Tel. 01953 860806

Unit	From	To	Aircraft	Squadron Code
453rd Bomb Group 732nd, 733rd, 734th, 735th Bomb Squadrons	22 December 1943	9 May 1945	B-24H/J/L/M Liberator	E3 F8 E8 H6

RACKHEATH (STATION 145)

Description: American bomber base used by the 467th Bomb Group in the Second World War.

Location: 5 miles north-east of Norwich.

Directions: Take the A1151 Wroxham road north-east of Norwich and the airfield is about 5 miles out on a right turn to

Overgrown tower at Rackheath – now restored. (Author)

Overgrown tower at Rackheath before restoration. (Author)

Rackheath. Turn left into Wendover Road (named after an air force base in the USA) on the Industrial Estate.
Comments: At the airfield little of the perimeter track, runways or hardstandings remain, and while the control tower stands derelict after being used as an office for a car breakers' yard for

Rackheath airfield with Sir Edward Stracey's estate in the foreground. (Author)

Rackheath Hall. (Author)

many years it is being restored to its original condition. Several
other wartime buildings, including a T2 hangar, remain and are
now used by local industry. The gymansium is now a storeroom
while the guardhouse is a furniture store. Little remains of the
living sites, communal site and sick quarters in the private
Rackheath Park opposite the airfield, which is accessible from

Rackheath airfield. (Author)

the Norwich–Wroxham road via the 'Golden Gates' (now almost gone). Charming gate houses, in pairs at the former rear entrance and the main, or 'golden' Gate's entrance are private residences. There is a private narrow winding concrete single-track road from the 'Golden Gates' to the late Sir Edward Stracey's Georgian manor house known as Rackheath Hall, which has been converted to apartments. Behind the house was an attractive lily pond and a clay tennis court which Sir Edward kindly allowed some 467th Bomb Group officers to use. A favourite feature of the property was a beautiful rhododendron drive. Enormous trees arched over a dirt road for 200 yards and created a fantastic tunnel of blossoms when in flower. Several barrack huts and air-raid shelters can be found in undergrowth throughout the park.

A memorial stone for the 467th Bomb Group was erected and dedicated in July 1990 on the airfield. The block has on its upper surface an outline plan of the airfield, together with 8th AF and 467th Bomb Group badges and the legend 'Rackheath Station 145'. On the front face is inscribed:

Traces of a B-24 crewman's 'bomb log' in a hut at Rackheath in 1999, which would have been kept near his bed. (Author)

Traces of a B-24 crewman's 'bomb log' in a hut at Rackheath in 1999, which would have been kept near his bed. (Author)

Crew 51's mission log painted on a SECO hut at Rackheath by
Sergeant Jack Hallman, a gunner in Eugene Garrett's crew.
(Author)

467th Bombardment Group Heavy, 2nd Air Division 8th Air Force, United States Army Air Force, under the command of Colonel Albert J. Shower, flew 212 combat missions, 5,538 aircraft sorties with losses of 235 airmen, 46 aircraft, in B-24 Liberator bombers from this airfield from March 11th 1944 to July 5th 1945. Over 5000 American airmen stationed here made a major contribution to the defeat of Nazi Germany in World War II. The Four Hundred and Sixty Seventh Bombardment Group Heavy Association Ltd.' The memorial was unveiled by 80-year old Colonel Albert J. Shower on 29 July 1990.

In Rackheath village near a crossroads on the Salhouse Road is Holy Trinity Church, outside of which near the village sign are two wooden benches dedicated in 1983. The village sign includes a picture of a Liberator. Beneath is a plaque, which reads. 'Dedicated 8 October 1983 to the memory of our comrades who died in training and in 212 combat missions flown in B-24 Liberator bombers from Station 145, Rackheath, Norfolk, England from 10 April 1944 to 25 April 1945 and to all assigned or attached to the 467th Bombardment Group (Heavy).' A Liberator and the group's Liberandos' badge also appear on the plaque. Pilot James G. Coffey and his crew presented the wrought iron gates and fence for the church and community centre and the plaque records their names, home towns and crew functions.

In the village church at Kirby Bedon, 3 miles south-east of Norwich, on a minor road off the A146 to Beccles, is a plaque 'to the memory of four gallant American airmen of the 8th Air Force who lost their lives when a Liberator bomber returning from a raid on Germany crashed near this church on August 18 1944. The parishioners of Kirby Bedon placed the memorial here. ' "Let us have faith that right makes might and in that faith let us, to the end, dare to do our duty." Abraham Lincoln.' The B-24 *Broad and High* in the 788th Bomb Squadron, flown by Roger L. Leister, had been hit by flak and crash-landed 2 miles from the church, where it hit an earth bank and disintegrated. A local farmer used four horses to help extricate the trapped co-pilot. Leister recovered from his injuries and went on to complete thirty-five missions. The plaque was dedicated on 29 October 1944.

Unit	From	To	Aircraft	Squadron Code
467th Bomb Group 788th, 789th, 790th, 791st Bomb Squadrons	12 March 1944	5 July 1945	B-24H/J/L/M Liberator	X7 6A Q2 4Z

Seething (Station 146)

Description: American bomber base used by the 448th Bomb Group in the Second World War.

Location: 9½ miles south-east of Norwich, to the east of the B1332 Norwich–Bungay road and south of the village of Seething.

Directions: Using the B1332 from Norwich, pass through the villages of Poringland (4 miles), Brooke (6 miles) and Kirstead (7 miles). One mile south of Kirstead turn left into the minor road signed Seething. After 1½ miles this road skirts the southern end of the airfield. Coming from the north or south using the A146 proceed along the Loddon bypass and at the crossroads halfway along the by-pass, take the minor road signed Mundham and Seething. Proceed to Seething (2½ miles) and at Seething turn left taking sign to Hedenham. After 1½ miles the road skirts the

On final approach to land at Seething. (Author)

Aircraft silhouettes in a billet at Seething in May 1981. (Author)

Aircraft silhouettes in a billet at Seething in May 1981. (Author)

western edge of the airfield before meeting the road leading to Thwaite St Mary at a crossroads. Turn left and this road leads onto the southern part of the airfield.

Comments: The control tower was restored between 1985 and 1987 and in 1987 the Seething Control Tower Association was formed. The tower is now a museum and is open on the first Sunday of each month, May–October, admission free. On the airfield are two memorial stones dedicated to the 448th Bomb Group. One is situated on the site of the Waveney Flying Group's clubhouse and hangars and is dedicated to the men who lost their lives flying from the base. It was dedicated in 1984. The second stone is situated next to the tower itself and was dedicated in 1990. There is also a memorial stone in the parish churchyard at Seething. DO NOT PASS BEYOND THE FORMER CONTROL TOWER AREA WITHOUT THE PERMISSION OF THE WAVENEY FLYING GROUP - THE PRIVATE RUNWAY (the former main north-east–south-west runway) IS IN ACTIVE USE. Other wartime buildings surviving on the southern side of the airfield include headquarters and barrack buildings.

Unit	From	To	Aircraft	Squadron Code
448th Bomb Group 712th, 713th, 714th 715th Bomb Squadrons	30 November 1943	6 July 1945	B-24H/J/L/M Liberator	CT IG EI IO

SHIPDHAM (STATION 115)

Description: American bomber base used by the 44th Bomb Group in the Second World War.
Location: 3 miles south of East Dereham.
Directions: In Shipdham village, 5 miles south-east of Dereham is a sign to the airfield. The first entrance leads to Arrow Air Services flying club, situated on the north side, tel. 01362 821063, open 10.00 a.m. to dusk, licensed bar and restaurant).

Barracks block
ravaged by Old
Father Time.
(Author)

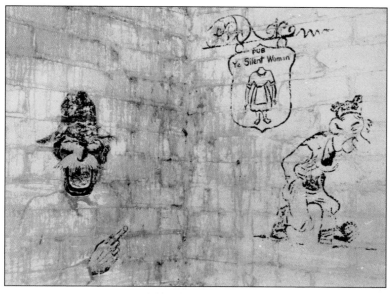

Norfolk yokel (laughing at Sad Sack leaving the pub) on a wall
at Shipdham in 1981. (Author)

Comments: Several industrial companies occupy the three
wartime T2 hangars on the south side where the technical site
was. The control tower has been partially restored, and though
far from complete, it is still standing. A plaque in memory of the
44th Bomb Group is affixed to the side of the tower. This was
donated in 1992 by First Lieutenant Robert Lee Aston, a navigator in the 67th Squadron and is inscribed with three B-24
Liberators, a plan of the airfield, and the insignia of the 44th
Bomb Group and 8th AF. A memorial to the 44th Bomb Group
is near the Arrow Air Services offices, and inside, near the reception area, is a museum display featuring photos and artifacts
relating to the 'Flying Eightballs.' On 3 September 1983, in All
Saints parish churchyard in Shipdham village, an inscription to
the 44th on the village war memorial and a granite memorial
were dedicated during a 44th Bomb Group veteran's reunion.
The granite memorial shows a plan of the airfield, a Liberator
and the 8th AF insignia, with the words:

Former 44th Bomb Group aircrew, L-R: Bob Bishop, Hap Westbrook and Joe Warth, at the dedication of the memorial to the 'Flying Eightballs' in All Saints parish churchyard in Shipdham village on 3 September 1983 during a 44th Bomb Group veteran's reunion. (Author)

Shipdham 44 BG. To those brave Americans who served and died in defense of their country and allies. In memory 44th Bomb Group (H) 1942–1945 United States Army Air Force.'

Near the Arrow Air Services offices on Shipdham airfield is a memorial stone to the 44th, inscribed:

8th Air Force B-24 Liberators. First mission 7 Nov 1942. Last mission 25 April 1945. Shipdham AAF Station 115. 'Flying Eightball Group'. 'Agressor beware'. 344 combat missions, 153 aircraft lost in action, 330 enemy planes destroyed. Awarded the Distinguished Unit Citation for Kiel Germany 14 May 1943, Ploesti, Romania 1 Aug 1943. Ready

Colonel Leon Johnson's fireplace in a hut at Shipdham in the 14th CBW area. (Author)

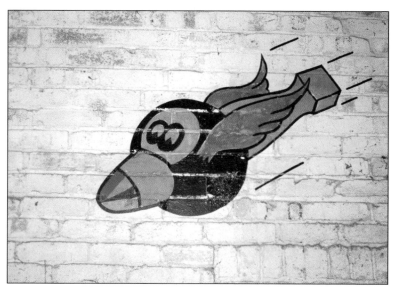

The 'Flying Eightball' insignia in a hut in the 14th CBW area. (Author)

'Hey Paw, tell me again how you and the boys were sweatin' it out in the ETO in England in 42, 43, 44, 45!' This mural is in a hut in the 14th CBW area. (Author)

Pin-up, one of several painted on walls at the 14th CBW HQ during the war by Jack Loman using paint bought at Jarrolds department store in Norwich in 1943. (Author)

Cartoon wolf and pin-up in a hut at Shipdham in the 14th
CBW area. (Author)

then–ready now–ready tomorrow. 44th Bomb Group (H),
Bomb Wing (VH), Strategic Missile Wing (SAC). Dedicated
by the 44th Heritage Memorial Group 24 September 1988.

Arrow Air Services maintain a small museum to the 44th Bomb
Group in their offices.

On dispersed sites to the south-east of the airfield several
wartime huts used as living quarters still stand. Several of these,
on the 14th CBW site, have been turned into private residences.
On the walls of some of the other huts, which are also on private
land, are paintings of pin-ups and cartoon characters like a
Norfolk yokel laughing at Sad Sack leaving the pub. There is a
multi-coloured 'Flying Eightball' insignia and a fantastic wall
mural showing a bar scene depicting a former 'Eightballer' who,
after returning to the USA is asked by his young son, 'Hey Paw,
tell me again how you and the boys were sweatin' it out in the
ETO in England in 42, 43, 44, 45!' Some of the paintings, which
were painted by Jack Loman using paint bought at Jarrolds
department store in Norwich in 1943, were reasonably intact in
2004 but the roof is missing from the hut containing the pin-ups
and cartoons and they will surely not survive too many more

Norfolk winters. One of the brick huts, that is being converted to a private residence, has a fireplace, which was built specially for Colonel Leon Johnson upon his return from Ploesti in August 1943. The morgue at the old ambulance station remains, standing alone and desolate in a field nearby. Watch out for rats!

Unit	From	To	Aircraft	Squadron Code
44th Bomb Group 66th, 67th, 68th, 506th Bomb Squadrons	10 October 1942	15 June 1945	B-24D/E/H/J/L/M Liberator	QK NB WQ GJ

TIBENHAM (STATION 124)

Description: American bomber base used by the 445th Bomb Group in the Second World War.

Location: North of the B1134 Pulham Market–New Buckenham road, known as Long Row, about 14 miles south of Norwich and 3 miles west of the A140 Norwich–Ipswich road.

Directions: From Norwich in the north, using the A140, pass through Long Stratton (10 miles) and after a further 3½ miles, at the crossroads with the B1134, turn right, taking the sign to Attleborough. Proceed along the B1134 and after 2½ miles pass over the railway level crossing and after a further ½ mile turn right off the B1134 taking sign Aslacton. After ½ mile, this road passes the eastern edge of the airfield and a private track, which leads to the Norfolk Gliding Club. Approaching from the south using the A140, 5½ miles beyond Scole, the crossroads with the B1134 is reached. Turn left and proceed as indicated above.

Comments: Only the west–east runway is incomplete; the main north-east–south-west runway is complete. Virtually none of the buildings remain; the modern housing development of Sneath Common is now on its site. If the private concrete road to the gliding club is used, on the right-hand side are the remains of the former administrative unit (now private farm buildings). The gliding clubhouse is situated on the site of one of the hangars and one of the former dispersal loops. A black marble memorial in memory of the 445th Bomb Group, unveiled during the 445th Bomb Group reunion on 25 May 1987, is located adjacent to the clubhouse. It has a view of a B-24 Liberator, the 8th AF insignia, a plan view of the airfield and the Circle 'C' fin code of the 445th Bomb Group. The wording reads:

445th Bombardment Group (H), 2nd Combat Wing, 2nd Air Division, 8th United States Air Force, 4th November 1943 to 28th May 1945. From this airfield the 445th Bombardment Group launched 280 missions and flew 6323 sorties. This memorial is humbly dedicated to the 445th Bomb Group in memory of those airmen who gave their lives and those who served fighting for the liberation of Europe during World War II. 700th BS. 701st BS. 702nd BS. 703rd BS. Dedicated 25th May 1987.

A small bronze memorial plaque was fixed to the internal wall opposite the main entrance to the Parish Church at Tibenham during the reunion in 1990. IF THIS PRIVATE ROAD IS USED VISITORS MUST REPORT TO THE GLIDING CLUBHOUSE. DO NOT GO ON THE RUNWAYS, THEY ARE STILL IN ACTIVE USE. Carrying on towards Aslacton, after passing the private entrance to the Flying Group, in ½ mile turn left. After ½ mile, the road passes the end of the airfield. A very impressive southward view is obtained of the main runway and the whole of the airfield. To the north are the remnants of the runway and perimeter track of the 1950s extension.

Unit	From	To	Aircraft	Squadron Code
445th Bomb Group 700th, 701st, 702nd, 703rd Bomb Squadrons	4 November 1943	28 May 1945	B-24H/J/L/M Liberator	IS MK WV RN

WATTON-GRISTON (STATION 376, REDESIGNATED STATION 505 IN JUNE 1943)

Description: Strategic air depot for the repair of 2nd Air Divison Liberators.

Location: Just to the east of the small town of Watton, Norfolk.

Directions: For Griston turn right off the A1075 Thetford–Watton road onto a minor road 2 miles before Watton.

Comments: The 250 acre airfield was built in 1938 and 1939 for the RAF, which operated Blenheims and other aircraft from the station until August 1942, when it was reallocated to the USAAF. Some of the most important but little-known units of the 8th AF were the strategic air depots assigned under the provisions of the Bradley Plan. These depots were responsible for the maintenance

B-24 42-52542 *Stinger* of the 791st Bomb Squadron, 467th Bomb Group that Lieutenant Thomas Murphy successfully crash-landed at RAF Watton on 8 May 1944 following damage sustained on the mission to Brunswick. (Wiley Noble)

and repair of combat aircraft. American Air Force (AAF) Station Watton-Griston in Norfolk was responsible for the maintenance and supply of the fourteen Liberator groups of the 2nd BD. The base was actually split between two units, the 3rd Strategic Air Depot (SAD) at Griston and the 25th Bombardment Group at the permanent RAF facilities at Watton. The 3rd SAD, comprising the 31st and 46th Air Depot Groups, was based at Watton from July 1943 and came under the control of 8th AF Service Command. To accommodate the 3rd SAD a vast township had to be constructed across the other side of the runway from Watton at Griston. It was called Neaton officially, but no community of that name existed. Plywood hutments, steel hangars and shops were constructed and the 3rd SAD utilized existing buildings, like the local church, which was used to conduct regular services together with the civilian services. Griston was adopted as the unit's home while Watton became AAF 376 with its one runway serving both the 3rd SAD and the 25th Bombardment Group.

In June 1943 active plans were laid to transform Watton-Griston into an 8th AF service command depot, redesignated Station 505. The 3rd SAD was responsible for the third- and fourth-echelon maintenance, plus all supply functions for the 2nd BD. The task was to salvage all Liberators which crashed in England. A field maintenance group went to every crash site and salvaged all parts that could be removed. Small mobile field units would go to sites of downed aircraft and if temporary repairs could be made on site, the Liberator would be flown back to

Watton for permanent repairs. Those aircraft beyond repair were transported by road to Watton after their lethal cargoes of bombs and ammunition had been removed. These teams always operated under very severe and primitive conditions. It was not uncommon for them to remain out in the field for several months at a time. Some were stationed at emergency landing strips at Woodbridge, Manston, Catfoss and any farmer's field where a Liberator might have come to rest. Every single item recovered was returned to depot stock for reissue to the combat groups.

The Bradley Committee recommended that the base air depots (Burtonwood, Watton, and Langford Lodge) would be called 1st, 2nd, and 3rd Base Air Depots. The intransit depots would be designated as strategic air depots. On 1 August 1943 there were four strategic air depots, located at Honington, Suffolk (1st SAD), Little Staughton (2nd SAD) Watton (3rd SAD) and Wattisham, Suffolk (4th SAD). Because of increasing needs and size of the strategic air depots, they were relocated in June 1944 at Troston (1st SAD), Abbots Ripton (2nd SAD), Griston (3rd SAD) and Hitcham (4th SAD). Towards the end of the war a fifth SAD was located in France.

The Americans took over Watton completely on 4 October 1943. In February 1944 the 3rd SAD began moving across to the

Celebrations at Watton-Griston in May 1945. (Wiley Noble)

Aerial view of Wayland Prison on the former Griston 3rd SAD
site at Watton-Griston. (Author)

The 3rd SAD
Memorial at
Griston (Author)

Griston site to make room for the 802nd Reconnaissance Group (P) commanded by Colonel Elliot Roosevelt. (On 9 August 1944 the 802nd was reactivated as the 25th Bomb Group and became part of the 325th PRW. The 25th Bomb Group's aircraft operated from Watton until almost the end of the war.) With the coming invasion and the subsequent increase in missions the 3rd SAD was called upon to make additional efforts. During the week ending 14 June the 3rd SAD Transport Division hauled 3,600 tons of materiel, mostly high explosive, for the 2nd BD groups.

The Griston site is now HM Prison Wayland. The prison chapel has a memorial tablet to the RAF and USAAF units that operated from the former airfield. In Griston parish churchyard is a black granite memorial to the 3rd SAD. The inscription reads: '3rd Strategic Air Depot World War II United States Army Air Force. A tribute to the American airmen who served their country and its allies by maintaining the B-24 Liberator bombers of the Eighth Air Force. 1943-Watton-Griston 1945.' The twenty-two sub-units of the 3rd SAD are listed on the outline shape of a B-24 fin and rudder. The memorial was dedicated on 9 June 1984. At the entrance to the prison, in a garden of remembrance, is a large granite memorial in a natural and irregular shape, which was dedicated by 3rd SAD veterans and their friends on 10 May 1995. The 3 ton granite stone was obtained from another prison in south-west England and transported to Griston. An inscription says 'At this site 4800 USAAF airmen of the Third Strategic Air Depot maintained the B-24 Liberator bombers of Eighth Air Force, World War II.'(There is also a memorial stone to the 25th Bomb Group just inside the main gate on the main B1108 Watton–Norwich road. On the station itself is a propeller memorial erected in May 1990 for a Blenheim unit of the RAF at Watton early in the war.)

Unit	From	To	Aircraft	Squadron Code
802nd Reconnaissance Group (P), 25th Bomb Group, 652nd, 653rd, 654th Bomb Squadrons	22 April 1944	23 July 1945	DH Mosquito XVI, B-17G, B-24D/H, B26G Marauder	
3rd Strategic Air Depot, 31st and 46th Air Depot Groups, 8th AF Service Command.	July 1943	July 1945	Maintenance and supply of the 14 B-24 Groups of the 2nd AD	None

WENDLING (STATION 118)

Description: American bomber base used by the 392nd Bomb Group in the Second World War.

Location: 4 miles west-north-west of East Dereham and north of the A47 trunk road in the parish of Beeston.

Directions: Taking the A47 Norwich – King's Lynn road eastbound, take a right turn about 7 miles before Dereham onto a minor road for Crane's Corner and Beeston industrial area.

Comments: Although most of the runways and some of the perimeter track survive, no wartime buildings remain on the airfield site. Several large sheds for turkey rearing stand on the runways. On the dispersed sites towards Beeston are Quonset huts and other structures. On a wall in what was the ground officers' mess, now a Jaguar car spares depot, a large mural showing a spread eagle and Liberators in flight all in blue is in good condition. The mural was revealed when a false wall was removed where the American bar had been. In other rooms there are traces of the black mission board, pin-ups, the outline of a P-47 and other items. In the doorway of the customers'

Aerial view of Wendling airfield in 1997. (Author)

Ground Officer's mess at Wendling in 1944. This building, which is now used by a Jaguar car spares business and which contains the B-24 silhouettes and eagle, was occupied by the Gilbert family just after the war when they were evacuated to the airfield after being  bombed out in Norwich during the Baedeker Blitz. (via Ben Jones)

Eagle mural in the ground officers' mess at Wendling in 1986. (Author)

Target list for 392nd Bomb Group at Wendling in 1981.
(Author)

entrance to the spares depot is a propeller blade from one of two B-24s of the 466th Bomb Group (H), which crashed after colliding, just after take-off from Attlebridge in bad weather on 27 March 1944.

A section of the firing butts remains. The obelisk memorial to the 392nd Bombardment Group, which stands in a formal garden near Beeston was paid for by the group and was unveiled on 2 September 1945. A plaque reads:

Dedicated to the men of US Army Air Forces Station No. 118 who through their efforts, devotion and duty, aided in bringing victory to the Allies in World War No. 2. 392nd Bombardment Group (H) Headquarters, 576th Bombardment Squadron (H), 577th Bombardment Squadron (H), 578th Bombardment Squadron (H), 579th Bombardment Squadron (H) of the United States Eighth Air Force. 465th Sub-Depot (Class I), 10th Station Complement Squadron, 1217th Q.M. Service Group (RS), 1825th Ordnance S & M Co. (Avn), 1287th Military Police Det. 'A' 806th Chemical Co. (AO) Det. 'A', 568th Army Postal Unit, 208th Finance Detachment, 210lst Eng-Fire-Fighting Platoon of the United States Eighth Air Force.

In 1989 repairs and alterations were made at the memorial site which was taken over by the US Battle Monuments Commission and a new plaque was added, reading: '392nd Bomb Group, 8th Air Force, US Army Air Forces, Station 118 Wendling. In honour of 747 airmen who gave their lives and all who served with them at this base. July 1943–June 1945.' Many 392nd veterans and their wives and many local people attended the rededication on 7 October 1989.

Under the 'Photos-in-Pubs' scheme, there are copies of a picture of two B-24s, *Short Snorter* and *Rose of Juarez*, returning from operations in late 1943 with the Normandy coastline below, in the Ploughshare at Beeston and the Rose Cottage at Wendling.

Near the tower of All Saints churchyard in Upper Sheringham on the north Norfolk coast is a memorial to the crew of B-24H Liberator *Alfred*, which crashed near the spot on 4 January 1944 while returning badly damaged from a mission to Kiel. Second Lieutenant Colby A. Waugh and four of his crew were killed, while five survived. The memorial was dedicated on 7 May 1994.

On the wall of the lodge at the American Military Cemetery at Madingley, near Cambridge and in the Central Library at Cheshunt, Hertfordshire, are identical plaques dedicated by the residents of Cheshunt and Waltham Cross to Second Lieutenant John D. Ellis and crew of B-24 42-95023 in the 577th Bomb Squadron. On 12 August 1944 this crew 'sacrificed their lives to prevent their aircraft from crashing on our homes'. After colliding with B-17G *The Tomahawk Warrior* of the 398th Bomb Group from Nuthampstead (which crashed at Lude Farm, Loudwater east of High Wycombe, Buckinghamshire) the B-24 crashed on Albury Farm, just north of where the M25 motorway meets the A10. Bad weather during assembly had caused six B-24s of the 392nd to abort the mission to the German airfield at Juvincourt, France.

Unit	From	To	Aircraft	Squadron Code
392nd Bomb Group, 576th, 577th, 578th, 579th Bomb Squadrons	August 1943	June 1945	B-24H/J/L/M Liberator	CI DC EC GC

Wymondham USAAF Hospital
(77th and 231st Station Hospitals)

Description: USAAF hospital, one of a considerable number set up to care for the casualties of the 8th AF.

Location: 2½ miles south of Wymondham and 12 miles from Norwich close to the A11 at Morley St Botolph.

Comments: Between the wars, in the grounds of Morley Hall, on whose site Wymondham College now stands, was the Mid-Norfolk Golf Course. In 1939 the golf links were taken over for agricultural purposes. Then an emergency hospital, designed by the Ministry of Works and built under the Lend Lease arrangement, was constructed. On completion, the hospital was handed over to the Americans and it became the 77th Station Hospital.

It provided all medical care at station hospital level for ground and flying personnel of fifteen heavy-bomber bases, a fighter group and affiliated service organizations such as engineer, quartermaster and ordnance troops – an estimated total of 60,000 troops – in the vicinity. Most of the work of the Surgical Service was carried out on casualties from the bomb wings received at high altitude on missions over France, Holland, Norway and Germany. Sixty per cent of casualties resulted from flak, 15 per cent from cannon-shell fragments and the rest from crashes and accidents. The general age of patients was between eighteen and thirty, and almost all admissions were severe. Almost 80 per cent of wounds involved upper and lower extremities, 15 per cent the head and a small number the chest and abdomen.

From 6 March 1944, the 77th became a reconditioning centre for enlisted men and the 231st moved from Redgrave Park, Suffolk, to Morley. From March the hospital acted as a receiving hospital for air force casualties rushed direct from operational missions over Europe. On 29 May 1944 a telephone call was received stating that within twenty-four hours the hospital would have to expand from 834 beds to 1,254 in anticipation of the expected casualties from the D-Day landings. After the invasion of France, ground forces battle casualties were evacuated there. On 12 July medical supply personnel prepared 200 stretchers in two hours, ready for the first mass admission of battle casualties from a hospital train at Wymondham Station.

Eight hospital trainloads, 2,099 patients, were admitted to the hospital in 1944. Careful plans were made in advance, with the hospital Admissions Officer boarding the train at Cambridge and recording any necessary information about each patient before assigning them to a ward. In 1945 1,155 patients were evacuated to the hospital.

Derek Daniels was one of the local children who were entertained at a Christmas party in the Red Cross clubhouse at the 231st Base Hospital on 23 December 1944.

> They came and collected us from our homes in ambulances and took us back to the hospital where we had a great time. We saw a film show and were given toys and sweets galore (for in Morley as elsewhere we were only allowed two ounces a week, we were rationed, but not here!) There was candy as the Yanks called it and gum by the yard. The toys were fun – some having been made by the wounded men, while they were convalescing. Then we had an enormous feed to end the party. We had fish, chips, meat, pickles, mince pies, Christmas pudding, crackers, and for drink it was either Coca-Cola (American only in those days) or cocoa. We were on rations at home. We thought we were in Canaan as it were, for it was certainly a place which flowed with milk and honey.

The hospital closed at midnight on 8 June 1945. After the war it was first of all a transit camp for the Royal Norfolk Regiment and then two training colleges. When the colleges closed, Sir Lincoln Ralphs had the inspired idea of turning the site into a boarding school for Norfolk County Council. In 1991, this became a grant-maintained school. Please contact the Head of Resources and College Promotions (tel. 01953 605566) for an appointment to visit. Wymondham Museum includes a display on the 231st US Army Hospital.

2nd Bombardment/Air Division Order of Battle

2ND BOMBARDMENT DIVISION

(Activated as the 2nd Bombardment Wing, 7 June 1942.
Re-designated the 2nd Bombardment Division, 13 September 1943.
Renamed the 2nd Air Division on 1 January 1945)
(Old Catton, Norfolk 7.9.42, later to Horsham St. Faith and finally Ketteringham Hall,
December 1943-June 1945)

Major-General James P. Hodges   7 September 1942–1 August 1944
Major-General W. E. Kepner   1 August 1944–13 May 1945
Brigadier-General Walter R. Peck   13 May 1945–31 May 1945

2ND COMBAT BOMBARDMENT WING (H)

Activated as the 201st Provisional Combat Wing (HB) 25 March 1943.
Re-designated 2nd Combat Bomb Wing (H) 14 September 1943

Unit	Base	1st mission	
44th Bombardment Group (H)	Shipdham	7.11.42	(transferred to the 202nd Combat Bomb Wing (P) 2.9.43)
93rd Bombardment Group (H)	Hardwick	9.10.42	(transferred to the 20th Combat Bomb Wing (H) 13.9.43)
389th Bombardment Group (H)	Hethel	9.7.43	
445th Bombardment Group (H)	Tibenham	13.12.44	
453rd Bombardment Group (H)	Old Buckenham	5.2.44	

14TH COMBAT BOMBARDMENT WING (H)

Activated as the 202nd Provisional Combat Wing (HB) 3 September 1943.
Re-designated 14th Combat Bomb Wing (H) 13 September 1943

Unit	Base	1st mission	
44th Bombardment Group (H)	Shipdham	7.11.42	(transferred from the 201st Combat Bomb Wing (P) 2.9.43)
392nd Bombardment Group (H)	Wendling	9.9.43	
492nd Bombardment Group (H)	North Pickenham	11.5.44	(withdrawn from combat 5 August 1944)
491st Bombardment Group (H)	North Pickenham	2.6.44	(transferred from the 95th Combat Bomb Wing (H) 14.8.44)

20TH COMBAT BOMBARDMENT WING (H)

Activated 22 September 1943.

Unit	Base	1st mission	
93rd Bombardment Group (H)	Hardwick	9.10.42	(transferred from the 2nd Combat Bomb Wing (H))
446th Bombardment Group (H)	Bungay	16.12.43	
448th Bombardment Group (H)	Seething	22.12.43	
489th Bombardment Group (H)	Halesworth	30.5.44	(transferred from the 95th Combat Bomb Wing (H) 14.8.44)

95TH COMBAT BOMBARDMENT WING (H)

Activated 11 December 1943.

Unit	Base	1st mission	
489th Bombardment Group (H)	Halesworth	30.5.44	(transferred to the 20th Combat Bomb Wing (H) 14.8.44)
491st Bombardment Group (H)	Metfield	2.6.44	(transferred to the 14th Combat Bomb Wing (H) 14.8.44)

96TH COMBAT BOMBARDMENT WING (H)

Activated 8 January 1944.

Unit	Base	1st mission
458th Bombardment Group (H)	Horsham St. Faith	24.2.44
466th Bombardment Group (H)	Attlebridge	22.3.44
467th Bombardment Group (H)	Rackheath	10.4.44

Bibliography

Bailey, Mike with Tony North, *Liberator Album: B-24s of the 2nd Air Division USAAF* Midland Publishing 1998

Benarchik Mike, *In Search of Peace*, 453rd Bomb Group History.

Bowman Martin W., *Fields of Little America* (GMS) 2001

Bowman Martin W., *Echoes of East Anglia* (Halsgrove Publishing Ltd) 2006

Bowman Martin W., *The B-24 Liberator* (PSL) 1989

Bowman Martin W., *USAAF Handbook 1939-1945* (Sutton) 2003

Bowman Martin W., *8th Air Force At War* (PSL) 1994

Bowman Martin W., *Great American Air Battles* (Airlife) 1994

Bowman Martin W., *Four Miles High* (PSL) 1992

Bowman Martin W., *Airfield Focus 53: Hethel* (GMS) 2002

Bowyer, Michael J. F., *Action Stations 1: East Anglia* (PSL) 1990

Congdon, Philip, *Behind the Hangar Doors* (Sonik)

Fairhead, Huby and Tuffen, Roy, *Airfields and Airstrips of Norfolk and Suffolk* (Norfolk and Suffolk Aviation Museum)

Fairhead Huby and Collis, Bob, *Airfield Focus 4: Horsham St Faith* (GMS) 1992

Ferguson, Andrew, *389th Bomb Group – Hethel* (Lotus Cars, unpublished,) 1992

Francis, Paul, *Military Airfield Architecture From Airships to the Jet Age* (PSL) 1996

Freeman, Roger, *Airfields of the Eighth Then and Now* (After the Battle) 1978

Freeman, Roger, *The Mighty Eighth in Colour* (Arms & Armour Press) 1991

Freeman, Roger, *The Mighty Eighth* (Macdonald) 1970

Healy, Allan, *The 467th Bombardment Group* (Privately printed) 1947

Innes, Graham Buchan, *British Airfield Buildings of the Second World War* (Midland) 1995

Innes, Graham Buchan, *British Airfield Buildings Expansion and inter-War Periods* (Midland) 2000

Kibble-White David H., *Airfield Focus 55: Rackheath* (GMS) 2002

Kibble-White David H., *Airfield Focus 57: Tibenham* (GMS) 2003

Lande D. A., *From Somewhere in England* (Airlife) 1991

Mahoney James J. and Mahoney Brian H., *Reluctant Witness* (Trafford Publishing) 2001

Marriott, Leo, *British Military Airfields Then and Now*, (Ian Allan Publishing) 1997

McKenzie, Roderick, *Ghost Fields of Norfolk* (Larks Press) 2004

Reynolds, George A., *Folded Wings of the 458th Bombardment Group* (Privately Published) 2001

Smith David J., *Britain's Memorials and Mementoes* (PSL) 1992

Smith, Graham, *Norfolk Airfields in the Second World War* (Countryside) 1994

South Norfolk Council, *USAAF Airfields in South Norfolk* (South Norfolk Council Unpublished)

Spencer, Ronald D., *There we were . . . or The saga of Crew No. 8* (Manuscript)

Tays R. H., *Country Boy, Combat Bomber Pilot* (Privately published) 1990

Walker, Peter M., *Norfolk Military Airfields* (Privately published) 1997

Wickham, Dick, *The War at My Door*